BAYESIAN STATISTICS

NINTH ANNUAL PHI DELTA KAPPA
SYMPOSIUM ON EDUCATIONAL RESEARCH

SPONSORED BY
PHI DELTA KAPPA

Syracuse University Chapter of Phi Delta Kappa
School of Education, Syracuse University

BAYESIAN STATISTICS

EDITED BY

DONALD L. MEYER
Syracuse University

RAYMOND O. COLLIER, JR.
University of Minnesota

F. E. PEACOCK PUBLISHERS, INC.
ITASCA, ILLINOIS

Library of Congress Catalog Card Number 75–86199

Symposium Participants

Chairman: Donald Meyer
SCHOOL OF EDUCATION
SYRACUSE UNIVERSITY

Presenting Papers

Jerome Cornfield, *University of Pittsburgh*
Bruce M. Hill, *University of Michigan*
Dennis V. Lindley, *University College, London*
Seymour Geisser, *State University of New York at Buffalo*
Colin L. Mallows, *Bell Telephone Laboratories, Incorporated*

1968–70 Officers of Phi Delta Kappa

Published Phi Delta Kappa Symposia on Educational Research

First Annual Phi Delta Kappa Symposium on Educational Research (University of Virginia, 1959)

Research Design and Analysis (Second Symposium on Educational Research—University of Minnesota, 1960)

Dissemination and Implementation (Third Symposium on Educational Research—The University of Oregon, 1961)

Simulation Models for Education (Fourth Symposium on Educational Research—Indiana University, 1962)

Education and the Structure of Knowledge (Fifth Symposium on Educational Research—University of Illinois, 1963)

The Training and Nurture of Educational Researchers (Sixth Symposium on Educational Research—The Ohio State University, 1964)

Improving Experimental Design and Statistical Analysis (Seventh Symposium on Educational Research—University of Wisconsin, 1965)

Learning Research and School Subjects (Eighth Symposium on Educational Research—University of California, Berkeley, 1966)

PREFACE

The Ninth Annual Phi Delta Kappa Symposium on Educational Research was held at Syracuse, New York, on January 12, 1968.

Because of the nature of the topic to be discussed, the format of the Symposium was altered in the following way. Each of the five presenters was asked to prepare his paper in advance for predistribution to the other panel members. The papers were not read at the meeting, but rather the available time was devoted to discussion of the papers, in particular, and of Bayesian philosophy and methodology, in general.

A number of questions and reactions to the papers were solicited in a somewhat informal way prior to the Symposium. We feel that this format makes good use of time, but we should have been more formal in assigning responsibilities for questions.

The discussion ran for the complete day. Minor editing on the part of the participants was allowed with the Editors being more severe, principally in deleting sections judged by them to be of lesser value for inclusion in this book.

Mrs. Ada Kornmuller typed and retyped in her usual efficient way and deserves our thanks.

August, 1969

Donald L. Meyer
Syracuse, New York

Raymond O. Collier, Jr.
Minneapolis, Minnesota

CONTENTS

1. The Frequency Theory of Probability, Bayes' Theorem, and Sequential Clinical Trials 1
Jerome Cornfield
University of Pittsburgh

2. Some Contrasts Between Bayesian and Classical Inference in the Analysis of Variance and in the Testing of Models 29
Bruce M. Hill
University of Michigan

3. Bayesian Analysis in Regression Problems 37
Dennis V. Lindley
University College London

4. Discriminatory Practices 57
Seymour Geisser
State University of New York at Buffalo

5. Some Comments on Bayesian Methods 71
Colin L. Mallows
Bell Telephone Laboratories, Incorporated

Discussion 85

References 127

Index 133

1

THE FREQUENCY THEORY OF PROBABILITY, BAYES' THEOREM, AND SEQUENTIAL CLINICAL TRIALS

BY JEROME CORNFIELD

UNIVERSITY OF PITTSBURGH

1. INTRODUCTION

My assignment today is both to give some broad general indication of what distinguishes the Bayesian outlook and to give some examples of what this outlook has to offer to those engaged in the planning, conduct and analysis of clinical trials. The present heavy involvement of statisticians and statistical ideas in clinical trials starts with the British Medical Research Council (MRC) and Sir Austin Bradford Hill. Earlier examples can of course be adduced. Karl Pearson had a long-continuing and polemical disagreement with Almroth Wright about the design of trials of typhoid vaccine. Nineteenth-century statisticians and probabilists, including Venn, were interested in appraising the effectiveness of Lister's methods. And in the eighteenth century D'Alembert and Bernoulli were interested in the possible effects of vaccination against smallpox on the overall death rate. The MRC's involvement was not casual, but total, however. It insisted on defining the questions to be answered, the evaluation procedures to be used, the patient population to be studied and many other scientifically important, although perhaps mathematically shallow, aspects of clinical trials. Its influence was sufficiently profound so that no less a person than the President of the Royal College of Surgeons could say recently that "the controlled clinical trial, which was developed by Sir Austin Bradford Hill . . . was as important and valuable (a contribution to medicine) as the discovery of penicillin." (Atkins [1966].)

The MRC also introduced to such trials certain theoretical ideas that were current in statistical circles in the 1930's. Some of these, such as randomized allocation of patients among treatments, are of permanent value. Others, particularly the doctrine that the conclusion to be drawn depends not only on the observations but on the sequential path leading to them, have been a serious bar to developing the flexibility in execution required in scientific experimentation. This latter doctrine is furthermore strongly qualified, if not entirely rejected, by Bayesian theory. Inflexibility and statistical rigor are no longer synonymous, as the following sections attempt to illustrate.

2. THE LONG-RUN FREQUENCIES OF ERRORS OF INFERENCE

Statistical theory starts with the key notion that we observe random variables, whose probability distribution is determined by a state of nature, but that we do not observe the state of nature itself. Any conclusions or decisions that are based on such observations must take account of their variable nature, i.e., of the fact that if repeated, the observations would be different. A seemingly natural way to implement this notion, and one which underlies the frequentist viewpoint which dominated statistics for the first half of this century, is as follows: we visualize first a probability model. This makes precise exactly how the observation would vary for any given state of nature. Thus, consider a population of sick patients, of whom proportion p might be cured by some new therapy. The proportion p is unknown to us and is an instance of an unknown state of nature. We decide to treat a sample of n patients and observe the number cured. The number is a random variable denoted by t. Then under reasonable sampling assumptions the probability distribution of t is given by the binomial distribution

$$\frac{n!}{t!(n-t)!}p^t(1-p)^{n-t} . \tag{2.1}$$

Secondly, we visualize a well-defined inference or decision procedure. That is to say, that even before any observations are made, we are prepared to state exactly what inferences or decisions any possible hypothetical values of these observations, i.e., realizations of the random variable, would lead to. For example, suppose some existing form of therapy leads to some known proportion cured, say p_1, and we are prepared to replace it by the new therapy only if we have strong evidence that it is better. Thus, we might insist the observed value of t, say t_0, be so high as to make it almost certain that the cure rate with the new therapy, p, is in fact higher than the old cure rate, p_1. A standard way of making this idea precise, given the frequency point of view, is to perform a test of the hypothesis that the new therapy was no better than the old one, i.e., that $p = p_1$. Call this hypothesis H_1. One asked for the probability of observing a number cured as high as or higher than the number observed, t, if the new cure rate, p, was in fact equal to the old rate, p_1, i.e., if H_1 was true. Only if this probability was suitably small, say equal to or less than α, would the old therapy be rejected. One was thus led to the decision rule: reject the old therapy if and only if the probability of observing a t at least as large as that observed was no larger than α, when $p = p_1$, or more concisely,

$$\text{Reject } H_1 \text{ if and only if } \sum_{r=t_0}^{n} \binom{n}{r} p_1{}^r (1 - p_1)^{n-r} \leq \alpha \; . \qquad (2.2)$$

The example is, of course, oversimplified. In practice one would want to test old and new therapy concurrently; one would want to consider other features of the therapy in addition to the cure rate, such as side effects, costs, etc. It does nevertheless highlight some essential features of the frequency viewpoint, in particular the attractive feature of having all entities operationally defined. Thus the probability α is simply the long-run proportion of times the hypothesis H_1 would be rejected if true. By setting low values of α, experimenters could control their error rate and give quantitative precision to the notion "almost certain." Furthermore, if one questioned the apparently commonsense notion of rejecting H_1 if and only if the observed number cured exceeded some given quantity and asked if a different decision rule might be better, the frequentist had an apparently overwhelming reply.

The argument begins by noting that if the new form of therapy were better, then there is some cure rate, $p_2 > p_1$, that obtains. Call the hypothesis that $p = p_2$, H_2. Then if H_2 is true and H_1 is not rejected, an error has been committed. There are in fact two types of errors. They are Type I: rejecting H_1 when true; Type II: not rejecting H_1 when false and H_2 is true. The probability of the first is no greater than α.

A little reflection shows that the probability of the second is given by

$$\sum_{r=0}^{t_0-l} \binom{n}{r} p_2{}^r (1 - p_2)^{n-r} . \qquad (2.3)$$

This probability, usually denoted by β, is simply the long-run relative frequency with which the second type of error would be committed. The frequentist concludes his argument by producing a mathematical proof of the proposition that of all tests of H_1 based on the random variable t leading to a Type I error of α or less, the test given by (2.2) leads to the smallest β. Whether H_1 or H_2 is true, that test will therefore lead to the smallest long-run frequency of errors and hence is to be preferred.

3. IDENTIFYING THE LONG RUN

In trying to apply this elegant and attractive approach one is saddened to find, however, that it is necessary to specify in which long run one regards one's particular result as embedded, and that this entails some unexpected and unwelcome consequences. A simple example will illustrate the difficulty. A scientist, having made n observations in the expectation that they would permit the rejection of a particular hypothesis at some predesignated significance level, say .05, finds that he has not quite attained this level. He still believes the hypothesis is false and asks a statistician how many more observations would be required to have reasonable certainty of rejecting the hypothesis. Suppose the statistician advises him on some basis or other to take m additional observations and that the result of the $n + m$ combined observations permits the rejection of the hypothesis at the desired significance level. A happy ending. Or is it? There are clearly two different long runs, of which the particular observation might be considered a member. The first consists of a series of hypothetical repetitions, each of size $n + m$, but with the particular observation, say proportion cured, varying from repetition to repetition. In this long run, the observation, or a more extreme one, would occur with probability .05 or less, if the hypothesis is true.

But there is another long run of which the observation can be considered a member. Each member of this long run consists of two stages of experimentation. At the end of the first, which is of size n, a test is performed. If significance is achieved, the experiment is terminated and the result announced. If not, a second stage, whose size depends on the first-stage result, is undertaken, and the combined results again examined. The long run here consists of a series of hypothetical repetitions, in which both the size of the experiment and the observation vary from repetition to repetition. But in this sequence of repetitions the particular observation, or a more extreme one, would, in contrast to the first sequence, necessarily occur with probability of .05 or more, if the hypothesis is true.

That this must be true is easy to see. If the hypothesis being tested is true, there is a .05 chance of rejecting it after the first stage. To this chance must be added the probability of rejecting after the second stage, given failure to reject after the first, and this increases the total chance of rejection to above .05. In fact, if the number of observations in the second stage is very large relative to the first, the actual significance level is .0975 ($= .05 + .95 \times .05$), if both first- and second-stage tests are performed at the .05 level.

If the first long run is regarded as appropriate, the observation permits rejection of the hypothesis, but if the second long run is so regarded, the hypothesis cannot be rejected, no matter how much additional evidence is gathered in the second stage. But surely, one might say, there can be no question of the appropriateness of the two-stage long run, since this in fact corresponds to the procedure actually followed. However, there are two consequences to this attitude. First, since for the second long run rejection at the .05 level is impossible, no matter what the second-stage results, no purpose can be served by taking further observations. The statistician whose advice was sought, and who took this position, would therefore be compelled to advise that further study was fruitless and that the scientist would best turn his attention to other matters. Secondly, if we consider another scientist, who had originally decided to take $n + m$ observations in one stage and had exactly the same results as the first scientist, he could reject the hypothesis in question while the first could not. The conclusion therefore depends not only on the evidence but also on the path by which it was reached. Both conclusions—that no amount of additional second-stage observation could strengthen the evidence against H_1 beyond a certain point and that the conclusion depends on both the path by which the evidence was arrived at and the evidence itself—would be surprising to many scientists, and, when clearly understood, probably unwelcome.

The dependence of the inference on the particular long run considered appropriate leads to serious difficulties in the conduct and interpretation of real clinical trials. Often, despite simple initial objectives, unforeseen complications develop and the questions that one started out to answer become modified. If realistic adjustments to such unforeseen complications are made during the course of the trial, the appropriate long run becomes so complicated that even an approximate frequency analysis of results becomes impossible. Because of this, many statisticians and some clinicians who have absorbed the frequency viewpoint regard it as desirable as a matter of principle to withhold results until the trial has been completed according to its original plan. Only in this way can one be sure of being able to answer the initial question, with the only undesirable consequence of such behavior being that, because of the unforeseen complications that develop, the initial question may no longer be of interest. To some statisticians and many clinicians such behavior has seemed like a caricature of real scientific method.

4. LONG-RUN FREQUENCY OF ERRORS AND WEIGHT OF EVIDENCE

These unexpected and unwelcome consequences of applying the frequency point of view stem from identification of the significance level, which is a measure of the long-run frequency of Type I errors, with a somewhat different concept, the weight of the evidence against the hypothesis being tested. In fact, the fundamental but unstated postulate on which much frequentist analysis of data is based is that "all hypotheses rejected at the same critical level have equal amounts of evidence against them." That this postulate is not as reasonable as it might at first sight appear is suggested by the following example, which is a modification of one originally due to Cox (1958). In this example a test of the hypothesis that a mean is zero against a particular alternative will sometimes reject the hypothesis when the observed value is zero. Furthermore, this test has virtually zero Type II error ($\beta < .000003$). By any possible definition of weight of evidence, however, it is clear that an observation of zero is evidence for the hypothesis and not against it. If a test with minimum Type II error leads to an opposite conclusion, then one cannot equate the concept of choosing between hypotheses on the basis of evidence and the concept of rejecting at a fixed significance level with minimum Type II error.

The example follows. We wish to test at the .05 level the hypothesis H_1 that the mean of a normal population is zero against the alternative, H_2, that the mean is 10. The observation, t, comes from one of two populations, and once the observation has been made it is known from which population it comes. The first population is normal with a standard deviation of 10 and the second is normal with a standard deviation of 1. Under H_1 both populations have mean 0 and under H_2 mean 10. The probability that the observation comes from the first population is .05 $- \epsilon$ and from the second .95 $+ \epsilon$, where

$$\epsilon = .95 \int_{4.5}^{\infty} (2\pi)^{-\frac{1}{2}} e^{-u^2/2}\, du \Big/ \int_{-\infty}^{4.5} (2\pi)^{-\frac{1}{2}} e^{-u^2/2}\, du$$

$$= .000003 \;. \tag{4.1}$$

A physical rationalization of this model is that the measurement is made using one of two unbiased measuring instruments, one of which has measurement error expressed by $\sigma = 10$ and the other by $\sigma = 1$, and that the measuring instrument is chosen at random with the stated probabilities.

We define the rejection region for H_1 to consist of the two events E_1 and E_2, where E_1 consists of the event t from the second population and $t > 4.5$, while E_2 is the event t from the first population for all t, including $t = 0$. The probability that either E_1 or E_2 will occur if H_1 is true is .05. Thus,

$$P(E_1|H_1) = (.95 + \epsilon) \int_{4.5}^{\infty} (2\pi)^{-\frac{1}{2}} e^{-t^2/2}\, dt \tag{4.2}$$

$$= \epsilon \;.$$

$$P(E_2|H_1) = .05 - \epsilon \;, \tag{4.3}$$

so that

$$P(E_1|H_1) + P(E_2|H_1) = \text{probability of a Type I error}$$

$$= .05 \;. \tag{4.4}$$

To obtain β we note that when H_2 is true and the mean is 10 the probability that the observation is from the second population and exceeds 4.5 so that H_1 is rejected is

$$(.95 + \epsilon) \int_{4.5}^{\infty} (2\pi)^{-\frac{1}{2}} e^{-[(t-10)^2]/2}\, dt \tag{4.5}$$

and is easily shown to exceed .95. The probability that it comes from the first population, so that H_1 is rejected, is .05 $- \epsilon$. The sum of the two probabilities gives the probability of rejecting H_1 when H_2 is true and exceeds $1 - \epsilon$. The complement gives the probability of a Type II error and is thus less than ϵ.

I shall return to this example in section 7 and show how a test more nearly in accord with the primitive idea of weight of evidence can be obtained.

5. BAYES' THEOREM

We now consider an alternative formulation of the idea of inference or weight of evidence. From the frequency point of view we consider the probability of observations, given the hypothesis, but we are in fact interested in the probability of the hypothesis, given the observation. But if probability is considered merely as a long-run relative frequency this latter concept is meaningless. Either the hypothesis is true, in which case its probability, considered as a long-run relative frequency, is 1, or it is false and its probability is 0. Unfortunately we don't know which.

A way out of this impasse is provided by considering an alternative, nonfrequency, interpretation of probability. But we first need some terminology and notation. Consider first a set of possible hypotheses, an instance of which is provided by H_1 and H_2 of the previous section. More generally, let us consider m possible hypotheses $H_1, H_2 \ldots H_m$. Secondly, consider a set of possible observations or outcomes, an instance of which is provided by the number of successes, t, of section 2. We shall assume t can take on n different values and shall denote them by $t_1, t_2 \ldots t_n$. We shall also assume that for each of the mn combinations of hypotheses and outcomes it is possible to calculate the direct probability of an outcome, given a hypothesis. This probability is denoted by $P(t|H)$ which is read as "the probability of the outcome t, given the state H." An instance of such a probability is given by equation (2.1).

For what follows we need a word which can be interpreted to mean either an outcome or a hypothesis. We shall use "proposition" in this sense. Consider now the collection of all possible propositions. We shall call this the proposition space and any particular proposition a point in the proposition space. The propositions are considered mutually exclusive in the sense that in any particular instance one and only one can be true. To each possible proposition a probability is "assigned." The idea of assigning a probability is the mathematician's trick to avoid considering the relationship between physical reality and his concepts and to confine his discussion to the formal properties of the concepts and to their implications. Since he does not pretend to any special competence in assessing physical reality, but does in deducing formal implications, this self-imposed restriction is understandable.

Thus, two tosses of a coin in which one observes only whether each toss is a head or a tail leads to a proposition space with four points

$$TT, TH, HT, HH \ .$$

To each of these points a probability is assigned. There is no inherent mathematical necessity that each point be assigned the probability 1/4. A consideration of how one would decide what these probabilities should be, whether from arguments of symmetry or from experience with many coin tosses (and if the latter, how one would justify the assumption that what has occurred in the past will continue to occur in the future), clearly takes a nonmathematical character which it is best to postpone until the purely mathematical questions have been disposed of. We accordingly let ourselves be temporarily taken in by the mathematician's trick of assigning probabilities and concern ourselves only with their formal properties.

The formal properties assigned to a probability are usually motivated by a reference to relative frequencies, and we shall temporarily go along with this. The properties may be summarized as follows: Denoting the possible mutually exclusive propositions by

$$A_1, A_2 \ldots A_k$$

we assign to each point a quantity $P(A)$ to be read as "the probability of A." The function $P(A)$ has three properties

$$0 \leq P(A) \leq 1 \ . \tag{5.1}$$

The composite event "A_1 or A_2" is called the union of A_1 and A_2. Thus, a tail on the first toss is the union of the propositions TT and TH. The second property of the function $P(A)$ is that

$$P(A_1 \text{ or } A_2) = P(A_1) + P(A_2) \ . \tag{5.2}$$

Let S be the composite outcome: A_1 or A_2 or $\ldots$ A_k. The third property of the function then is

$$P(S) = 1 \ . \tag{5.3}$$

The fourth and final property to be defined is that of conditional probability. Let there be two classes of propositions, A and B. The class A could, for example, consist of the two possible propositions: an individual (1) has or (2) has not developed lung cancer during some defined time interval. The class B could similarly consist of the two possible propositions: an individual is examined and found to be (1) a cigarette smoker or (2) a noncigarette smoker. Generalization of what follows to more than two possibilities is immediate. In this situation the proposition space consists of the four points

$$A_1B_1, A_1B_2, A_2B_1, A_2B_2 ,$$

where A_1B_1 denotes the composite proposition both A_1 and B_1, and is identical with the proposition B_1A_1. Note that A_1 and B_1 are not mutually exclusive, since an individual can both have developed lung cancer and be a cigarette smoker. The functions $P(A_1)$ or $P(B_1)$, the unconditional probabilities of developing lung cancer or of being a cigarette smoker, are defined by properties (5.1), (5.2), and (5.3). It is also desirable, however, to talk about the conditional probability of developing lung cancer, given that one is a cigarette smoker. We denote this probability by $P(A_1|B_1)$ and define it as follows:

$$P(A_1|B_1) = P(A_1B_1)/P(B_1) . \tag{5.4}$$

From the relative frequency point of view this definition has the following simple motivation. $P(B_1)$ represents the proportion of individuals who are cigarette smokers, $P(A_1B_1)$ the proportion who are both cigarette smokers and have developed lung cancer, while their ratio represents the proportion of cigarette-smoking individuals who develop lung cancer.

From these four defined properties we can deduce Bayes' theorem almost trivially. From (5.4), dropping the subscripts, we have by symmetry

$$P(B|A) = P(BA)/P(A) = P(AB)/P(A)$$

so that

$$P(AB) = P(A)P(B|A) . \tag{5.5}$$

Similarly, B is the union of the mutually exclusive events $A_1B, A_2B, \ldots$ so that $P(B) = P(A_1B \text{ or } A_2B \text{ or } \ldots)$. It is easy to deduce from (5.2) that

$$P(A_1B \text{ or } A_2B \text{ or } \ldots) = P(A_1B) + P(A_2B) \ldots$$

so that

$$P(B) = \sum_i P(A_iB), \tag{5.6}$$

while from (5.5)

$$P(A_iB) = P(A_i)P(B/A_i) . \tag{5.7}$$

If we now use (5.5) to rewrite the numerator of (5.4) and (5.6) and (5.7) to rewrite its denominator we have

$$P(A|B) = \frac{P(B|A)P(A)}{\sum_i P(B|A_i)P(A_i)}. \tag{5.8}$$

This is Bayes' theorem. It expresses the conditional probability of A, given B as a function of the conditional probability of B, given A, and of the unconditional probability of A.

To tie this up formally with the hypotheses and possible outcomes with which we started we now make the purely notational change of replacing the propositions $A_1, A_2 \ldots$ by the hypotheses $H_1, H_2 \ldots$ and the propositions $B_1, B_2 \ldots$ by the outcomes $t_1, t_2 \ldots$ We may then rewrite (5.8) as

$$P(H|t) = \frac{P(t|H)P(H)}{\sum_i P(t|H_i)P(H_i)}. \tag{5.9}$$

Bayes' theorem thus provides an expression for the conditional probability of hypothesis H, given the outcome, t, as a function of the conditional probability of the outcome, given the hypothesis and the unconditional probability of the hypothesis. The left-hand side of (5.9) is often called the posterior or a posteriori probability of H, and the quantity $P(H)$, the prior or a priori probability of H.

There are occasions in which the use of a finite number of hypotheses is restrictive. Thus, in the binomial example of section 2 it is less natural to say that the possible hypotheses are cure rates of $p_1, p_2 \ldots p_m$ than to say that the cure rate can take on any real value between 0 and 1. Removal of this restriction complicates the argument mathematically but results in no basic change in ideas. Thus, $P(H|t)$ is changed only by substituting an integration over a continuous hypothesis space for the summation shown over the finite space and is interpreted as a probability density.

To provide an interpretation other than a frequency one to the quantity $P(A)$ defined by (5.1), (5.2), (5.3), and (5.4) we start with remarks by Ramsey (1926) that a "probability of 1/3 is clearly related to the kind of belief which would lead to a bet of 2 to 1" and "having degrees of belief obeying the laws of probability implies a further measure of consistency, namely such a consistency between the odds acceptable on different propositions as shall prevent a book being made on you." The idea behind the second remark is as follows. Suppose you are a bookmaker who posts odds on all the events on which you are willing to bet. You are willing to take either side.

Consider the events "rain tomorrow" and "no rain tomorrow." Suppose you offer 4 to 1 against the former, i.e., act as if its probability were .2 and act as if the probability of the latter were .3. Operationally this means that to anyone who bets 20 cents on "rain tomorrow" you pay one dollar if it does rain and nothing if it doesn't. Clearly anyone can make book against you if these are your assignments by betting both 20 cents on rain and 30 cents on no rain. No matter what happens you must pay out one dollar and therefore are certain to lose 50 cents. Your odds are inconsistent, or as De Finetti (1937), who independently developed the same idea, termed it, incoherent. What properties must be satisfied by the odds, or the probabilities to which they are convertible, to be coherent, i.e., prevent book from being made on you? Both Ramsey and De Finetti showed that it is necessary and sufficient that they possess the properties (5.1), (5.2), (5.3) and (5.4). There is thus no formal reason why probabilities need be interpreted as frequencies. Finally, Savage (1954), in a work that is largely responsible for the current revival of interest in Bayes, showed that the notion could be generalized beyond that of consistent betting behavior. It is thus possible without mathematical contradiction to talk about the probability of a hypothesis, given observations. All we need recognize is that the probability need not have a frequency interpretation.

It is useful to conclude this section with an example of the application of Bayes' theorem. Most texts on probability give one. The following, taking off from a puzzle of Gardner (1961), may prove amusing as well as instructive.

Three men, A, B and C, are under sentence of death. The governor decides to pardon one of them. He writes their names on three slips of paper, shakes the slips in a hat, draws out one slip, and communicates it to the warden. Rumors of this reach A, who tries, unsuccessfully, to persuade the warden to disclose the name. The warden does agree, however, to give the name of a prisoner, other than A, who will be executed. Specifically,

(*a*) if A is the one pardoned, he will flip a coin to decide whether to name B or C.

(*b*) if A is to be executed, he will name the other one to be executed.

The warden concludes that no information will be supplied by such a statement, and, after leaving, so that A cannot see whether or not a coin has been flipped, sends word that B will be executed. A reasons that since either he or C must be the other to be executed, his probability of being the one pardoned has now increased to 1/2. Is he right, or is the warden the better probabilist?

From the formalism of Bayes' theorem, we have three hypotheses:

H_1	A is to be pardoned
H_2	B is to be pardoned
H_3	C is to be pardoned

Because of the random choice of the governor's, $P(H_1) = P(H_2) = P(H_3) = \frac{1}{3}$. We also have the observation t, consisting of the warden's statement, "B will be executed." To calculate $P(H_1|t)$ we need $P(t|H_1)$ for $i = 1, 2, 3$. But by the conditions agreed to

$$P(t|H_1) = \tfrac{1}{2};\ P(t|H_2) = 0;\ P(t|H_3) = 1, \text{ so that}$$

$$P(H_1|t) = \frac{(\frac{1}{2})(\frac{1}{3})}{(\frac{1}{2})(\frac{1}{3}) + (0)(\frac{1}{3}) + (1)(\frac{1}{3})} = \tfrac{1}{3}\,.$$

The warden is therefore correct, since A's posterior and prior probabilities are the same. One can also calculate that $P(H_2|t) = 0$ and $P(H_3|t) = \frac{2}{3}$, so that the warden's statement does convey information about B and C, but of course his statement was made only to A. In Gardner's version of the problem, A communicates with C by tapping in code on a water pipe. But this only demonstrates that the warden was a poor penologist. Perhaps, like Newton, he was appointed to his post for his purely mathematical accomplishments.

Finally, we remark that a frequency interpretation of sorts can be given to this problem by imagining a large sequence of random selections of the man to be pardoned by the governor. In the long run generated by this sequence, we can select out those cases in which the warden says "B will be executed." Then the long-run relative frequency with which A will be the one to be executed in this subsequence will be $\frac{1}{3}$, $\frac{2}{3}$ for C, and 0 for B. Thus, the Ramsey-De Finetti-Savage interpretation of probability is not an alternative to a frequency interpretation but a generalization of it, applicable both when frequency interpretations are possible and when they are not.

6. LIKELIHOOD FUNCTIONS AND THE EFFECT OF STOPPING RULES

I now consider whether the function $P(H|t)$, given by Bayes' theorem, provides a measure of the weight of evidence which takes care of the difficulties considered in sections 3 and 4. To do this, I must first introduce the notion of a likelihood function. Roughly speaking the likelihood function is that part of $P(t|H)$ which depends on H. We make this a little more precise by returning to (2.1). This probability is a particular case of $P(t|H)$, with t being the number of cures and H being the hypothesis that the cure rate is p. Note that the expression can be written as the product of two factors, one of which, $n!/t!\,(n-t)!$, does not depend on p and the other of which, $p^t(1-p)^{n-t}$, does. The second factor is an instance of a likelihood function. To clarify this further we note that (2.1) can be obtained by assuming n independent trials at constant probability, p, with the long run consisting of repetitions, always of n trials, with only the number of cures, t, varying from one repetition to another. Suppose we were told, however, that this was not really the long run that had produced the observation and that in fact the sampling scheme had been to continue sampling, like Diogenes looking for honest men, until some specified number t was obtained. In that case the long run consists of repetitions, always with t cures, but with n, the number of trials necessary to achieve t cures, varying from one repetition to another. If the trials are independent and at constant probability p, then it is an elementary exercise to show that the probability of stopping after examining n patients is

$$\frac{(n-1)!}{(t-1)!(n-t)!}\,p^t(1-p)^{n-t}\,. \tag{6.1}$$

This is not the same as the probability (2.1). Thus, for $p = \frac{1}{2}$, $n = 2$ $t = 1$, the $P(t|H)$ given by (2.1) is $\frac{1}{2}$, but for the second $\frac{1}{4}$. The two likelihoods are the same, however.

Suppose now we compute $P(H|t)$ from (5.9), first using the $P(t|H)$ given by (2.1) and then the $P(t|H)$ given by (6.1). Evidently the factor that does not depend on H can be taken outside the summation or integration over H and cancels the same factor which appears in the numerator. Thus, $P(H|t)$ depends only on the likelihood function and not on the full probability. Furthermore in this particular case the likelihood function does not depend on which long run we consider the result as embedded in, so that $P(H|t)$ is the same whichever sampling scheme was actually followed. All that matters is that in n patients, t cures were observed, and it does not matter whether n or t was fixed in advance.

Clearly $P(H|t)$ depends on the evidence only to the extent to which the evidence affects $P(t|H)$, and in fact it depends only on that part of $P(t|H)$ given by the likelihood function. Finally, for the example considered the likelihood function does not depend on the stopping rule. Can one be sure this will always be the case? Anscombe (1953) first showed in complete generality that this was always the case, and the likelihood function does not depend on the stopping rule. Except therefore for the practically unimportant case of "informative stopping rules" (a lucid exposition of which has been given by Roberts [1967]), $P(H|t)$ is independent of the stopping rule. The hypothetical scientist of section 3 with his two-stage procedure can thus reach a conclusion which depends only on his observation t and which is independent of the number of stages by which he arrived at it. More generally, in medical or other experimentation there is no reason why one cannot adjust to unforeseen complications, since such adjustments will have at most an easily calculated effect on the likelihood function and hence on $P(H|t)$, and to the conclusions drawn from observations. The doctrine that all observations leading to the same likelihood function will lead to the same conclusions about H is called the likelihood principle.

7. BAYESIAN CHOICE BETWEEN TWO HYPOTHESES

Choice between two hypotheses is a problem of ancient vintage in statistical theory, even though attempts to apply it to practical situations characterized by a multiplicity of hypotheses can lead to seriously misleading results, as is apparent in many efforts to apply some procedures stemming from Wald's sequential analysis to clinical trials (Cornfield [1966]). We nevertheless consider such choice because it helps clarify the relationship between Bayesian and frequentist outlooks and because it incidentally illuminates the Cox example of section 4. It is sometimes claimed, or at least implied, by frequentists that, in contrast to Bayesians, they seek rules which minimize the long-run frequency of errors of inference or decision. If Bayesian procedures really lacked this property, then it would be difficult to accept them or to make them the basis of any scientifically defensible system of data analysis or behavior. We shall here argue that no such contradiction exists.

One simple way of choosing between two alternatives is to accept H_1 if $P(H_1|t) \geq$ some constant, say $c(0 \leq c \leq 1)$ and to accept H_2 if it is not (see, however, section 10). It is easy to see that if we let

$$R(t) = \frac{P(t|H_1)}{P(t|H_2)} \tag{7.1}$$

that this is equivalent to accepting H_1 if

$$R(t) \geq \text{some constant, say } \lambda \tag{7.2}$$

where

$$\lambda = \frac{c}{1-c} \Big/ \frac{P(H_1)}{1 - P(H_1)}$$

and H_2 if not. Since a constant independent of H appears in both numerator and denominator of the right-hand side of (7.1), it cancels out, and $R(t)$ depends only on the ratio of likelihood functions and is independent of the stopping rule.

Can anything be said about the long-run frequency of errors implied by the rule (7.2) in view of the fact that the rule does not depend on which long run generated t? Recalling the α and β of section 2 (i.e., the long-run relative frequency with which H_1 is rejected when H_2 is true and with which H_2 is rejected when H_1 is true), it is clear that α and β depend individually upon the long run which generated t and that therefore nothing can be said about them. An important result due to Savage and Lindley (Savage [1964]) says, however, that no matter what the long run the rule (7.2) is necessary and sufficient to minimize a linear compound of them, namely $\alpha + \lambda\beta$. The positive quantity λ can then be interpreted as the weight one would be willing to assign to Type II as compared to Type I errors. As the frequency outlook is usually applied, a standard α, such as .05 or .01, is selected and then a rejection region is sought which minimizes β, and this seems to be what is meant by references to the error-minimizing properties of frequency procedures. This treats the two types of errors in an asymmetric way. Whether one can operationally justify such an asymmetric treatment or not, it is nevertheless clear that the selection of a rejection region as in (7.2) also has error-minimizing properties.

Can any justification be given for choosing a rejection region as to minimize a linear rather than a nonlinear combination of α and β? The Savage-Lindley argument depends on the notion that two rejection regions, one of which, R_1, say, has a smaller α and the other, R_2, say, a smaller β, may be equally acceptable. Then it is reasonable to postulate that the rejection region formed by choosing R_1 with probability p and R_2 with probability $1 - p$ will be as acceptable as R_1 and R_2. This postulate implies indifference curves which are linear and parallel, and it leads directly to the minimization of a linear function of α and β.

Consider the application of the rejection region (7.2) to the Cox example. $R(t)$ is given by the ratio

$$e - [t^2 - (t - 10)^2]/2\sigma^2 \qquad (7.3)$$

where $\sigma = 10$ if t comes from the first population and $\sigma = 1$ if it comes from the second. This is equivalent to the rule:

$$\text{reject } H_1 : \mu = 0 \qquad \text{if and only if} \qquad t > 5 - (\log_e \lambda)\frac{\sigma^2}{10}. \qquad (7.4)$$

The critical values leading to rejection of H_1 for various values of λ and σ are shown below:

λ	*t from* *first population* ($\sigma = 10$)	*second population* ($\sigma = 1$)
0.5	11.93	5.07
0.67	9.05	5.04
1.00	5.00	5.00
1.50	0.95	4.96
2.00	−1.93	4.93

If both errors are regarded as equally important ($\lambda = 1$), the critical value is 5 whether t comes from the first or the second population and H_1 is not rejected when $t = 0$. If the Type II error is regarded as 50 percent more important ($\lambda = 1.5$), the critical value is 4.96 for $\sigma = 1$ and .95 for $\sigma = 10$. These critical values are appropriate no matter what the probabilities of t coming from the first or second population. This corresponds to common sense which says that no matter what the circumstances that led to making the measurement, the only appropriate evidence for choosing between H_1 and H_2 is the observation t and the knowledge of which instrument it was made with.

The α and β do depend on the probabilities of coming from the two populations. These are shown below for various values of λ using (7.2).

λ	α	β
0.5	.006	.029
0.67	.009	.023
1.00	.016	.016
1.50	.023	.009
2.00	.029	.006

Although the β are larger than those for section 3, the α are smaller and, of course, $\alpha + \lambda\beta$ is no greater than $.05 + .000003\,\lambda$ for all λ.

8. A WORD ON PRIOR PROBABILITIES

To compute $P(H|t)$ given by Bayes' formula in (5.9) one needs essentially two quantities, $P(t|H)$ and $P(H)$. The assignment of the former quantity often presents no difficulty in principle. Its determination may require a considerable past experience and will be subject to all the usual difficulties and problems of observational science—definition of the conditions under which the observations are repeatable, etc. But it is a fact of scientific experience that these difficulties can often be surmounted and assignments on which fairly general agreement exists can be obtained. The assignment of the prior probabilities, $P(H_i)$ has presented more of a problem, however. In fact the delay in the publication of Bayes' original paper until after his death was apparently due to his unresolved doubts about this assignment. Certainly much of the disagreement, past and present, about the applicability of Bayes' theorem to real problems, particularly scientific ones, has turned on the question of how to assign the priors. At one time it was thought that some unique formal expression of ignorance about possible hypotheses would lead to such assignments, but this view is not now widely held. A more common view would be that expressed by Mosteller and Wallace (1963) in their application of Bayesian methods to the study of disputed authorship of 12 of the Federalist papers.

> Prior distributions are not of major importance. While choice of underlying constants (choice of prior distributions) matters, it doesn't matter very much, once one is in the neighborhood of a distribution suggested by a fair body of data. We conclude from this that the emphasis on the difficulty, even impossibility, of choosing prior distributions as a criticism of the use of Bayes' theorem is not well placed.

This attitude, which is shared by most Bayesians, amounts to rejecting the doctrine that a given set of data leads to a unique inference. In the next three sections I shall try to indicate how this somewhat relaxed and nondogmatic attitude towards priors has led to progress in our understanding of and ability to analyze problems arising from clinical trials.

9. ON SAMPLING TO A FOREGONE CONCLUSION

Concern that the likelihood principle may entail a disregard for the consequences of the inferential procedure used is most forcibly expressed in the problem of sampling to a foregone conclusion (Anscombe

[1954], Robbins [1952]). We imagine an investigator (hypothetical, of course) with a strong prejudice against the hypothesis H_1, that the mean of normal population θ has value zero, and who wishes to amass evidence that will support this prejudice. He decides to make sequential observations on the normal random variable x, where $Ex = 0$ and $Ex^2 = 1$, and to compute

$$t_n = \frac{1}{n}(x_1 + x_2 + \ldots + x_n) , \tag{9.1}$$

for $n = 1, 2, \ldots$. He adopts the following stopping rule:

$$\text{if } |t_n| < k/n^{\frac{1}{2}}, \text{ he takes another observation;} \tag{9.2}$$

but

$$\text{if } |t_n| \geq k/n^{\frac{1}{2}}, \text{ he stops,} \tag{9.3}$$

where $k > 0$.

After stopping, he interprets the inequality (9.3) as providing strong evidence against H_1—the larger the value of k, the stronger the evidence. His argument is that the likelihood of H_1 relative to the likelihood of the hypothesis $\theta = t_n$ is low, in fact no greater than $e^{-k^2/2}$ and that H_1 is therefore inconsistent with the evidence. Alternatively, if a normal prior with variance well in excess of unity is assigned to θ, then the posterior probability that θ is zero or has a sign opposite to that of t_n will be small for large k, and again the inequality (9.3) might be considered as providing strong evidence against H_1.

But as several authors have pointed out, the probability that the inequality (9.3) will eventually be realized is, by the law of the iterated logarithm, essentially unity, even when H_1 is true. Thus, if one accepts the likelihood principle and the irrelevance of the stopping rule, one must also accept as evidence against H_1 observations that one is virtually certain to obtain when H_1 is true. If this is not an actual logical contradiction, it is uncomfortably close to one. Nor can it be dismissed by reference to the asymptotic nature of the law of the iterated logarithm, since, as Armitage (1967) has shown, the probability of realizing the inequality (9.3) can be substantial even for finite n. In view of this result, one must again ask whether the likelihood principle can be reconciled with concern for probabilities of incorrect conclusions. If it cannot, the flexibility provided by the likelihood principle may have been purchased at too high a price.

But if one is concerned about the high probability of rejecting H_1 if observation is continued until (9.3) is satisfied, it must be because some possibility of the truth of H_1 is being entertained. An appropriate formal expression of such concern is provided by assignment of a nonzero prior probability to H_1. But the use of any smooth and bounded prior probability distribution function is equivalent to the assignment of zero probability to H_1 and does not provide an expression of this concern. In fact the apparent justification for sampling to a foregone conclusion provided by the likelihood principle is entirely a consequence of assignment of zero probability to H_1 and is eliminated by assignment of a nonzero probability, no matter how small.

To show this we introduce a prior probability function for θ, namely,

$$P\{\Theta = 0\} = p \ ,$$

$$P\{\theta \leq \Theta \leq \theta + d\theta\} = \frac{1-p}{\sigma}\phi[\theta/\sigma]\,d\theta \qquad \text{for } \theta \neq 0 \ , \tag{9.4}$$

where

$$\phi(x) = (2\pi)^{-\frac{1}{2}}e^{-x^2/2} \ . \tag{9.5}$$

Then, by Bayes' theorem the posterior probability that $\theta = 0$, given t_n, which we denote by $P\{0|t_n\}$, is given by

$$P\{0|t_n\} = \left[1 + \frac{1-p}{p(n\sigma^2+1)^{\frac{1}{2}}}\, e^{n^2\sigma^2 t_n^2 (n\sigma^2+1)}\right]^{-1} . \tag{9.6}$$

We see from (9.6) that differing from zero by k standard errors need no longer imply strong evidence against H_1. In fact, setting $n^{\frac{1}{2}}t_n = k$ in (9.6) we note that for any $p > 0$, we have $P\{0|t_n\}$ approaches unity as n increases. Thus, although there is unit probability that $|n^{\frac{1}{2}}t_n|$ will eventually exceed k, it no longer follows that there is also unit probability that $P\{0|t_n\}$ will eventually be less than any preassigned quantity.

But an even stronger conclusion is possible. Suppose an effort is made to disprove H_1 by adopting the following stopping rule.

$$\begin{array}{ll} \text{if} & \alpha_1 < P\{0|t_n\} \leq 1 \text{ take another observation} \\ \text{but if} & P\{0|t_n\} \leq \alpha_1 \text{ stop} \ , \\ \text{where} & 0 \leq \alpha_1 < p \ . \end{array} \tag{9.7}$$

If one stops at all, then it will be only when $P\{0|t_n\} \leq \alpha_1$, and H_1 hence is improbable. It is easy to show (Kerridge [1963]) that the probability of ever stopping, when H_1 is true, is less than or equal to $[\alpha_1/(1-\alpha_1)]/[p/(1-p)]$. Therefore, if one sets out to disprove H_1 by continuing observation until the posterior odds in favor of H_1 are only 100α percent of the prior odds, the chance of succeeding is at most α.

The introduction of a nonzero prior probability for H_1 thus eliminates the possibility of sampling to a foregone conclusion.

In practice how could values for the prior constants, p and σ in (9.6), be assigned? In many applications the conditional prior distribution of θ, given the falsity of H_1, will be quite diffuse, that is, σ may be quite large. But from equation (9.6) it is clear that

$$\lim_{\sigma\to\infty} P\{0|t_n\} = 1\,, \qquad \text{for all } p > 0 \text{ and } t_n\,, \tag{9.8}$$

so that we cannot simply assign σ an arbitrarily large value. The ratio of the prior probability assigned to H_1 to the prior probability density assigned to θ near H_1 is $p\sigma/(1 - p)$, and for large n the values of p and σ assigned affect $P\{0|t_n\}$ only through their effect on the quantity $p\sigma/(1 - p)$. As a preliminary to investigating sensitivity to choice of p and σ, it seems useful, therefore, to permit σ to become infinite, and p to go to zero, but in such a way that $p\sigma/(1 - p)$ remains fixed and equal to a constant c^{-1}. We then have from (9.6)

$$P^*\{0|t_n\} = \lim_{\substack{p\to 0\\ \sigma\to\infty}} P\{0|t_n\} = \left[1 + \frac{c}{n^{\frac{1}{2}}}\, e n t_n^2/2\right]^{-1}\,. \tag{9.9}$$

In situations in which such an assignment is appropriate the number of prior constants is then reduced from two to one. It is instructive to consider the interpretation of the prior constant, c. The limits on nt^2 implied by the stopping rule (9.7) with α_2 substituted for the right-hand value of unity are, using (9.9),

$$\text{lower: } \log n + 2\log\frac{1-\alpha_2}{\alpha_2 c}$$

$$\text{upper: } \log n + 2\log\frac{1-\alpha_1}{\alpha_1 c}\,. \tag{9.10}$$

But nt_n^2 is nonnegative, so that the smallest n for which the lower limit could possibly be reached is that value for which the lower limit has value zero. For smaller values of n, the lower limit is negative and $P^*\{0|t_n\} < \alpha_2$, even for $t_n = 0$. Denoting the value of n which makes the lower limit zero by n_0, we find

$$\frac{1-\alpha_2}{\alpha_2}\, n_0^{\frac{1}{2}} = c\,. \tag{9.11}$$

The constant n_0 is thus the smallest number of observations leading to zero mean that will lead to the acceptance of H_1 at posterior probability level α_2. It thus provides a convenient, and operationally interpretable, way of quantifying vague prior beliefs about H_1, when the conditional prior distribution of θ, given the falsity of H_1, can be taken as diffuse.

For a clinical trial of some new form of therapy an appropriate value of n_0 for $\alpha_2 = .95$, say, would rarely fall below 10 or rarely exceed 1,000, the lower value being perhaps reserved for forms of therapy suggested by others, and the upper for testing one's own ideas. The maximum effect of vagueness in prior beliefs on both upper and lower limits for nt_n^2 is thus, from (9.10) log 1,000 − log 10 or 4.6 for all α_1 and α_2. By contrast, the effect on the upper limit of raising $1 - \alpha_1$ from .95 to .99 is to raise it by 3.3 for all n. The arbitrariness introduced by the vagueness of prior beliefs about H_1 can thus reasonably be argued to be of the same magnitude as that involved in selecting a posterior probability level and a good deal less than that involved in specifying alternatives. The effect of n_0 relative to the effect of selecting a posterior probability level on the lower limit is larger. Nevertheless, the ambiguity introduced by vague prior probabilities does not appear to introduce any more qualitatively serious vagueness than is introduced by various uncertainties about the statistical model used or by various scientific uncertainties, such as choice of treatment schedule, type of patient, or stage of the disease.

10. AN ADAPTIVE PROCEDURE FOR SEQUENTIAL CLINICAL TRIALS

An adaptive decision process is one in which behavior at any stage in the process is modified by what has been learned at earlier stages. Although there are numerous ways in which adaptive processes might contribute to sequential clinical trials, as for example, in the determination of optimum dosage, the practice and much of the theory of such trials has been indifferent to the idea. Greenhouse, Halperin and myself in work as yet unpublished considered a particular adaptive process, namely one in which an increasing proportion of patients is assigned to the better of two treatments, as evidence for it accumulates. The approach is in the spirit of the two-armed bandit problem (Jacobs [1967]), the solution to which would involve assigning patients to one of two treatments in such a way as to maximize the number assigned to the better treatment. No analytical solution to this problem has been found and even numerical solutions are far beyond the capacity of existing computers.

An analytic solution for a much simplified version of the two-armed bandit problem has been considered by Anscombe (1963b) and by

Colton (1963). They postulated a two-stage trial. In the first stage equal numbers of patients are assigned to each of two treatments, while in the second all remaining patients are assigned to the apparently superior one. They sought an appropriate size for the first or data-gathering stage by minimizing the sum of the costs for the first and second stage. For fixed treatment effect, the cost was defined as proportional to the number of patients assigned to the inferior treatment at the first stage, and to the expected number of patients assigned to the inferior treatment at the second stage.

The adaptive process we consider is obtained by generalizing the Anscombe-Colton solution in three directions. (1) In their treatment a probability distribution with zero mean is assigned to the unknown treatment difference. We assume that before the data-gathering stage a prior distribution with nonzero mean can be assigned—on the basis perhaps of previously gathered data. (2) In the Anscombe-Colton model one half the patients in the data-gathering stage are assigned to each treatment, whereas in the generalization we assign arbitrary proportions, θ and $1 - \theta$ and determine θ, along with the other constants, so as to minimize cost. We refer to this cost-minimizing solution as the optimum two-stage allocation. (3) We apply this optimum two-stage solution in multistage fashion. At any given point in the sequential stream of patients we consider ourselves as about to embark on a new two-stage trial, with all previously obtained results used to determine the new prior distribution of the treatment difference. The θ that would minimize costs in this assumed two-stage procedure is then interpreted as the proportion of the next "small" batch of patients assigned to treatment 1. After those patients' results are available a new prior and a new θ are computed, etc.

Considered as a multistage procedure it is not optimum, since the successive θ's have been obtained assuming two stages, but then applied in a multistage fashion. It does lead, however, to lower costs than does the optimum two-stage procedure. This follows immediately from the optimality principle of dynamic programming which states, "an optimal policy has the property that whatever the initial state and initial decision are, the remaining decisions must constitute an optimal policy with regard to the state resulting from the first decision." Further and perhaps substantial reductions could be achieved with an optimum multistage solution.

The solutions for θ are shown in Table 1.1. We note first that for every finite R considered there is a constant, $k(R)$, such that for $\Phi(z) < k(R)$ the optimum solution consists of $\theta^* = 0$ for any p between

TABLE 1.1

VALUE OF θ^*, PROPORTION ALLOCATED TO THE APPARENTLY INFERIOR TREATMENT AS A FUNCTION OF $\Phi(z)$, THE PROBABILITY THAT IT IS INFERIOR, AND $R(= N\sigma_0^2/2\sigma^2)$.

	R								
$\Phi(z)$	.5	1	5	20	50	100	500	1,000	∞†
.001......									.003
.01									.036
.02								.027	.056
.025......								.041	.065
.050......							.074	.083	.101
.100......						.106	.139	.146	.157
.15					.149	.170	.194	.198	.209
.20				.170	.209	.225	.243	.246	.254
.25				.236	.263	.275	.289	.292	.299
.30			.218	.294	.313	.322	.333	.335	.340
.35			.299	.347	.361	.368	.376	.377	.381
.40		.264	.369	.399	.408	.412	.417	.419	.420
.45	.350	.390	.435	.450	.454	.456	.459	.459	.460
.50	.500	.500	.500	.500	.500	.500	.500	.500	.500

† $\theta^* = \alpha + \sqrt{(\alpha - 1)}$ for $z < 0$
$\theta^* = \frac{1}{2}$ for $z = 0$
where $\alpha = \Phi(z) + z^{-1}\phi(z)$.

z = Standardized mean of prior.
$\Phi(z)$ = Probability that the apparently inferior treatment is in fact better.
N = Total number of future patients to be treated.
σ_0 = Standard deviation of normal prior for treatment difference.
σ = Standard deviation of the normal variable measured for each patient in the trial.

Note: All blank entries are zero.

0 and $\frac{1}{2}$. The probability $\Phi(z)$ can be interpreted as a significance level. The constant $k(R)$ can then be interpreted as a critical level as it is sometimes used in practice, i.e., the level of evidence at which one is justified in stopping the collection of further data and acting on the evidence obtained. Table 1.1 indicates that this critical value is highly sensitive to the value of R, varying from something greater than .40 at $R = .5$ to less than .02 at $R = 1{,}000$. The common practice of treating some favorite critical value like .05 as a universal yardstick therefore receives no more support from this decision formulation than it has from any other. The solution $\theta^* = 0$ has a straightforward rationalization when N is small: namely, that so little additional information can be collected relative to what is already known that

one might as well stop further data collection and treat all remaining patients with what appears to be the best treatment. In a multistage application of this two-stage result σ_0^2 will decrease so that R can become small, even though N is large. An alternative rationalization of the solution $\theta^* = 0$ is then that even for large N one will discontinue further data collection for a given probability, $\Phi(z)$, as the evidence on which this probability is based becomes stronger. This contrasts with the criticism sometimes made that Bayesian procedures depend on probabilities, but not the reliability with which they are determined.

Application of these results might ease the ethical problem involved in trials on human subjects. The usual ethical justification for not administering an agent of possible efficacy to all patients is the absence of definite information about its effectiveness. However satisfactory this justification may be before the trial starts,it rapidly loses cogency as evidence for or against the agent accumulates during the course of the trial. But any solution, such as the present one, which permits adaptive behavior, i.e., the allocation of proportionately more and more of the future patients to the apparently better treatment, at least reduces this ethical problem. It is, of course, understood that any such solution, even an optimum multistage one, is to be interpreted as a guide and not an inflexible rule, since the full consequences of decisions may be beyond calculation.

11. UNANTICIPATED MULTIPLE COMPARISONS

The idea of a confidence region and of the simultaneous confidence limits on contrasts of interest has been the frequency theory's solution to the problem of multiple comparisons, anticipated or unanticipated. The basic notion has been that if one started out to compare two unknown normal means, μ_1 and μ_2, by observing the corresponding independently distributed sample means, $\bar{x}_1$ and $\bar{x}_2$, and in the process discovered that certain rearrangements of the data leading to $\bar{x}_3 \ldots \bar{x}_p$, also independent, suggested that some combinations of $\mu_3 \ldots \mu_p$ demanded attention, all was not lost. One could define a contrast $\sum_{i=1}^{p} \lambda_{ij}\mu_i$, where $\sum_i \lambda_{ij} = 0$ and a set of such contrasts by letting $j = 1, 2 \ldots$. For many particular sets of contrasts so defined it has been possible to find h_j such that

$$P\left\{-h_j \leq \sum_{i=1}^{p} \lambda_{ij}(x_i - \mu_i) \leq h_j\right\} = 1 - \alpha, \quad j = 1, 2 \ldots . \quad (11.1)$$

The set of statements inside the bracket is then a composite statement and the probability that one or more elements of it are in error is α. Thus if it turns out that one should be interested in more than $\mu_1 - \mu_2$, i.e., in more than the contrast defined by $\lambda_{11} = 1$, $\lambda_{12} = -1$, $\lambda_{1k} = 0$, $k = 3, 4, \ldots$ one could expand the set of contrasts by computing a new set of h_j. Of course, the larger the set of contrasts of interest the broader the limits on any particular contrast, so that the investigator who maintained a single-minded interest in $\mu_1 - \mu_2$ could determine it within narrower limits than the investigator who had wider interests but the same observations. This was usually explained as the "price" one paid for being interested in too wide a set of contrasts. Why there should be a price or why observations on $\mu_3 \ldots \mu_p$ should render one's conclusions about $\mu_1 - \mu_2$ less precise remained unclear. For a time there was a good deal of discussion as to whether the contrasts implied by the F test as delineated by Scheffé (1953) or by the studentized range as delineated by Tukey (1951), or a number of other suggested contrasts such as Dunnett (1955) and Halperin (1955) were most appropriate but, although multiple comparison procedures appear to retain some popularity, this particular question appears never to have been resolved. In fact, it is clearly recognizable as the often irresolvable question of which long run to regard the data as embedded in.

A possible Bayesian attitude towards these problems is illuminating. Let us start by assigning to $\mu_1 \ldots \mu_p$ common, independent normal priors with mean μ and variance σ_1^2. Consider independent, normal means, $\bar{x}_i$, such that $E\bar{x}_i = \mu_i$ and $V(\bar{x}_i) = \sigma_0^2/n_i$. Then it is a straightforward exercise to show that the mean of the posterior distribution of μ_i is

$$\left\{\frac{n_i\sigma_1^2}{\sigma_0^2}\bar{x}_1 + \mu\right\} \Big/ \left\{\frac{n_i\sigma_1^2}{\sigma_0^2} + 1\right\} \tag{11.2}$$

and its variance is

$$\left(\frac{n_i}{\sigma_0^2} + \frac{1}{\sigma_1^2}\right)^{-1} \tag{11.3}$$

Three unknown constants are involved in these expressions, the mean and variance of the assumed prior, μ and σ_1^2 and the variance of an observation, σ_0^2. Since Student's 1907 paper it has been realized that mathematically well-defined ways exist of treating problems in which σ_0^2 is unknown. A Bayesian solution to Student's original problem, the assignment of a uniform prior to log σ and integration over σ leads to Student's distribution. If the prior mean in (11.2), μ, is assigned a uniform prior and integrated out, a new normal prior results with mean of the same form as (11.2), but with the overall sample mean substituted for μ, and a variance somewhat larger than (11.3). The prior variance, σ_1^2, presents more of a problem, since the integration is not straightforward. Lindley (1962) substituted the sample estimate of the component of variance between means for σ_0^2 and showed that the resulting estimates of μ_i were uniformly superior to those supplied by just using $\bar{x}_i$ with respect to a mean square error criterion. More recently Box and Tiao (1967) have obtained a full Bayesian solution by assigning diffuse priors to the σ_1^2 and σ_0^2 and integrating them out. The result is not in principle different from that provided by Lindley's.

Clearly this approach provides an alternative solution to the multiple comparison problem. Thus, for p large it would be possible for the estimated component of variance to be quite small, so that essentially all μ_i were estimated as equal to the overall sample mean, even though one of the observed $\bar{x}_i$ was quite separate from the others. This estimate is in the spirit of distrust of isolated and unanticipated results that is shared by all good data analysts, whatever their theoretical persuasion, and which frequentist multiple comparison procedures attempted to formalize. Its basic difference from frequentist procedures is that the limits on μ_i are narrowed, and not widened, by using information on other means. In the limiting case when σ_1^2 is shown to be very large relative to $\sigma_0^2\mu_i$, the limits are the same as for the univariate case.

There is one unsatisfactory feature to this solution, which is worth brief discussion even though it becomes somewhat conjectural, since it takes us beyond the point of known mathematical results. Consider $\bar{x}_i$, $i = 1, 2 \ldots p$, with $p - 1$ of the $\bar{x}_i$ bunched together, one of them separate, and a between mean component of variance approximately equal to the σ_i^2/n_i. The above solution would move all p of the $\bar{x}_i$ an equal distance towards the common mean, if the n_i are all equal. This hardly seems reasonable. This suggests the desirability of complicating the structure of the priors by assigning $\mu_i, \mu_2 \ldots \mu_p$ a multivariable normal prior with the same means but an arbitrary covariance matrix. The means of the resulting posteriors then depend on this arbitrary covariance matrix. Diffuse priors for covariance matrices exist, however, and the possibility of integrating out the prior covariance matrix seems attractive and is in any event now under investigation. One might of course ask what information on such a covariance matrix can be supplied by observations on independent means which is equivalent to that supplied for μ, σ_1^2 and σ_0^2. A possible answer is supplied by the observation that the variance of a difference depends on both the variances and covariances, so that if μ_1, μ_2 and μ_3 all have the same variances and the data suggest that $\mu_1 - \mu_2 > \mu_1 - \mu_3$, this also suggests $\rho_{12} < \rho_{13}$.

12. MISCELLANEOUS

A constant theme throughout the examples considered in this paper has been the crucial dependence of frequentist procedures upon specification of the appropriate long run. It is remarkable that this weakness was clearly stated almost a half century ago by Keynes (1921). Thus,

> Whether or not the probability of a proposition is relative to given *data*, it is clearly relative to the particular class or series to which we choose to refer it. A given proposition has a great variety of different probabilities corresponding to each of the various distinct classes of which it is a member; and before an intelligible meaning can be given to a statement that the probability of a proposition is so-and-so, the class must be specified to which the proposition is being referred . . . . But, as a given proposition belongs to innumerable different classes, how are we to know which class the premisses indicate as appropriate? What substitute has the frequency theory to offer for judgements of relevance and indifference? And without something of this kind, what principle is there for uniquely determining the class, the truth-frequency of which is to measure the probability of the argument? Indeed the difficulties of knowing how given premisses determine the class of reference, by means of rules expressed in terms of previous ideas, and without the introduction of any notion, which is new and peculiar to probability, appear to me insurmountable.

Unsuccessful though Keynes' positive proposals were, the criticism of the frequency theory seems remarkably prophetic.

Finally, we note a limitation in principle with the application of Bayes' theorem which it shares with the frequentist outlook—and that is the specification of the hypothesis space. Given its specification, Bayes' theorem applies. But in fact the development of new hypotheses is an important scientific act—it often wins Nobel prizes—and it falls completely outside the scope of theorem. In this respect it is no different from mathematics itself, which is concerned with methods of proving theorems, but has no advice on how to formulate new ones. Perhaps not the least of the advantages of the Bayesian outlook therefore is that it provides a clear-cut distinction between creative activity such as hypothesis formulation, which can be performed only by trained and imaginative people, and formal analysis, which is in principle capable of reduction to routine performance by robots.

2

SOME CONTRASTS BETWEEN BAYESIAN AND CLASSICAL INFERENCE IN THE ANALYSIS OF VARIANCE AND IN THE TESTING OF MODELS

BY BRUCE M. HILL

UNIVERSITY OF MICHIGAN

1. SUMMARY

Bayesian inference in the random model analysis of variance is discussed. Under the usual model this inference contrasts greatly with classical inference when the usual unbiased estimator of the between variance component is negative. Such data may also, however, provide strong evidence against the usual model itself. The process of testing the usual model against a broadening in which residuals in the same row are negatively correlated is then examined and contrasted with some classical methods of testing models.

2. BROADENING THE USUAL MODEL

Suppose that an experimenter plans to collect data for which he anticipates that the usual random model of the analysis of variance will yield an appropriate analysis. By "usual random model" is meant the assumptions $y_{ij} = \mu + \alpha_i + \epsilon_{ij}$, with $\alpha_i \sim N(0, \sigma_\alpha^2)$, $\epsilon_{ij} \sim N(0, \sigma^2)$, and $(\alpha_i, \epsilon_{ij})$ independent, $i = 1, \ldots, I$, $j = 1, \ldots, J_i$. I do not mean to imply that the "true" distribution of the observations is that specified by the usual model, or even that there is anything like a "true" distribution, but merely that the experimenter judges that an analysis based upon the usual model is likely to be more fruitful and lead to more appropriate inference than an analysis based upon any other model he knows of. However, he is not pigheaded, and he withholds an epsilon of probability (whose precise value may not matter very much) that in fact the usual model may be quite inappropriate; he has even considered beforehand, at least roughly, the kinds of alternative models to which he attaches some credence, and the kinds of data which might force him to enormously magnify that epsilon in favor of one or more of the various alternative models. In short, he anticipates that the usual model will be appropriate, but is prepared to be surprised.[1] I shall shortly illustrate how a negative value of the usual unbiased estimator of the between variance component can force such an experimenter to abandon the usual model in favor of an alternative model with negatively correlated residuals. Before this can be considered, however, it is essential to understand the nature of inference about σ_α^2 under the usual random model.

Suppose for simplicity that the experiment is balanced, i.e., $J_i = J$ in which case $\hat{\sigma}_\alpha^2 = J^{-1}\ (MSB - MSW)$ is the usual unbiased estimator of $\sigma^2{}_\alpha^2$.[2] Let $\rho(\mu,\ \sigma^2,\ \sigma_\alpha^2)$ be a joint prior density function for μ, σ^2, σ_α^2. For a very wide class of such prior distributions, including those which in a natural sense represent "vague prior knowledge" and thus correspond to the classical statistician's notion of ignorance, the marginal posterior density of σ_α^2 is approximately proportional to $\rho(\sigma_\alpha^2)\ g(\sigma_\alpha^2)$, where $\rho(\sigma_\alpha^2)$ is the marginal prior density of σ_α^2, and $g(z)$ is the density of a random variable

$$Z \sim J^{-1}\left(\frac{SSB}{\chi^2_{(I-1)}} - \frac{SSW}{\chi^2_{I(J-1)}}\right),$$

with the chi-square random variables independent. Note that given the data, SSB and SSW are known constants, Z is a random variable whose distribution is parameterized by I, J, SSB, SSW, and Z is negative with positive probability. Since of course $\rho(\sigma_\alpha^2) = 0$ for $\sigma_\alpha^2 < 0$, the posterior distribution of σ_α^2 is in effect that of Z, weighted by $\rho(\sigma_\alpha^2)$, and truncated from below at zero. Now the density of Z

[1] It goes without saying that he cannot consider all eventualities, and would not, if he could. All that is required is a reasonable degree of foresight and preparation.

[2] I use here and throughout fairly standard notation. The reader can refer to my articles (Hill [1965] [1967]) for further details.

turns out to be unimodal, with the mode approximately at $\hat{\sigma}^2_\alpha$. Some reflection shows that if $\hat{\sigma}^2_\alpha$ is positive and not too small, and if $\rho(\sigma^2_\alpha)$ is suitably gentle near $\hat{\sigma}^2_\alpha$ and not too large elsewhere, then the posterior distribution of σ^2_α is approximately that of Z, truncated from below at zero. Bayesian inference about σ^2_α would then be based upon this posterior distribution. Thus $\hat{\sigma}^2_\alpha$ might be taken as a naïve guess at the value of σ^2_α, while the posterior probabilities of intervals containing $\hat{\sigma}^2_\alpha$ measure how close σ^2_α is likely to be to $\hat{\sigma}^2_\alpha$. In a practical sense Bayesian inference about σ^2_α in this case does not differ greatly from the inferences of Fisher and the Neyman–Pearson school. Indeed, Fisher proposed that the fiducial distribution of σ^2_α be taken as the distribution of Z, censored from below at zero, i.e., with the mass to the left of zero piled up at zero. For large $\hat{\sigma}^2_\alpha$ this is approximately the same as truncation, since the mass to the left of zero is negligible. Neyman–Pearsonites base inference upon the conditional distribution of $\hat{\sigma}^2_\alpha$, given σ^2, σ^2_α. Although exact confidence intervals are not available, approximate intervals agree fairly well with Bayesian credible intervals, provided $\hat{\sigma}^2_\alpha$ is large enough. Thus for such data all three methods of inference are in substantial agreement. Furthermore, our experimenter typically has no more reason to suspect the usual model a posteriori than he had a priori, so he uses it with good conscience, just as he had intended.

The case $\hat{\sigma}^2_\alpha < 0$ is very different. Since Z is unimodal with mode approximately $\hat{\sigma}^2_\alpha$, it is clear that $g(\sigma^2_\alpha)$ will typically be monotonically decreasing for $\sigma^2_\alpha \geq 0$ when $\hat{\sigma}^2_\alpha < 0$. Thus relatively more weight will be given to small σ^2_α in the posterior density, $\rho(\sigma^2_\alpha)\ g(\sigma^2_\alpha)$, than in the prior density, $\rho(\sigma^2_\alpha)$. However, as SSW grows large the function $g(\sigma^2_\alpha)$ becomes flat, and for virtually any proper prior density the posterior distribution of σ^2_α converges to the prior distribution. Thus data with large SSW are almost totally uninformative about σ^2_α from the Bayesian viewpoint, in sharp contrast with frequentistic views. I shall now give a brief proof of this result.

Let $n = SSW$, and $\gamma^2 = \sigma^2/n$. The posterior density of μ, γ^2, σ^2_α is then

$$\phi''_n(\mu, \gamma^2, \sigma^2_\alpha) \propto \gamma^{-IJ} \exp - \tfrac{1}{2}\gamma^{-2} \times$$

$$[1 + J\sigma^2_\alpha/n\gamma^2]^{-I/2} \exp - \left[\frac{SSB + IJ(\mu - \bar{y})^2}{2(J\sigma^2_\alpha + n\gamma^2)}\right] \rho(\mu, n\gamma^2, \sigma^2_\alpha)\ .$$

If there exists a constant K with $-\infty < K < IJ - 2$ and a sequence

$r_n > 0$ such that $r_n \gamma^{-K} \rho(\mu, n\gamma^2, \sigma_\alpha^2)$ is dominated uniformly in n by an integrable function of μ, σ_α^2, and if also $\lim_{n\to\infty} r_n \rho(\mu, n\gamma^2, \sigma_\alpha^2)$ exists and is equal to say $\rho^*(\mu, \gamma^2, \sigma_\alpha^2) > 0$, then it follows from the dominated convergence theorem that a limiting distribution of μ, γ^2, σ_α^2, exists as n goes to infinity, having density proportional to

$$\gamma^{-IJ} \exp - \tfrac{1}{2}\gamma^{-2} \rho^*(\mu, \gamma^2, \sigma_\alpha^2) \ .$$

Thus for sufficiently large SSW the data carry virtually no information about μ, σ_α^2! Note that the above proof does not go through for any improper prior density of the form $\rho(\mu, \sigma^2, \sigma_\alpha^2) \propto f(\sigma^2)(\sigma_\alpha^2)^{-1}$, since such a $\rho(\mu, n\gamma^2, \sigma_\alpha^2)$ is not dominated by an integrable function of μ, σ_α^2. This hardly disturbs me since I regard such improper prior distributions with some skepticism, and use them only with caution. In practice I believe the very modest condition on the prior density required in the proof will always be met.

The above conclusion contrasts with every frequentistic interpretation of negative $\hat{\sigma}_\alpha^2$ that I know of. Thus Fisher will have high fiducial probability that in fact $\sigma_\alpha^2 = 0$. Although exact Neyman–Pearson theory is nonexistent (as is typical in all but the most trivial problems of statistical inference), and although the approximate theory is a morass of muddled and disparate views, still the consensus of Neyman–Pearsonites seems to be that very negative $\hat{\sigma}_\alpha^2$ is strong evidence that σ_α^2 is small or even zero. Now since the three theories give such different results, it would seem that one should be able to demolish at least two of the theories, preferably the other two. Yet I must admit that I am unable to do so, not even in the highly artificial situation where the usual model is known to be valid. All I can do is hope that after reflection others will agree with me that the inference I have suggested is much the more reasonable of the three, given that the usual model holds. Of course the observation of an extremely negative $\hat{\sigma}_\alpha^2$ is quite extraordinary under the usual model. But I do not see how this at all affects the relevance of the comparison of the theories based upon such data. For such data can occur even under the usual model, and each theory should be able to suggest a reasonable inference given such data. Similarly, one does not contrast Newtonian and relativistic mechanics based upon the motion of everyday particles, but rather quite exotic ones. When the artificial assumption that the usual model is known to hold is dropped, then the inference, of course, becomes very different. Very negative $\hat{\sigma}_\alpha^2$ may now provide strong evidence against the usual model. This does not alter the truth of the previous inference, given that the usual model holds, and I believe that it is essential to understand the nature of inference under the usual model before one can intelligently consider whether or not to reject that model. Now let us consider a broadening of the usual model.

The specific extension that will be considered here is that in which a negative covariance, C, is possible between any pair of residuals in the same row. This is of course not the only possible broadening of the usual model. It is singled out here because there are many real situations in which I think it is not at all implausible, a priori, as I have argued elsewhere (Hill [1967]). For example such a covariance might arise from an inadvertently restricted sampling procedure. To simplify things I shall now assume that the sure event can be partitioned into two subsets (hypotheses) under which the two models hold.[3] Let A_0 denote a hypothesis under which the usual model holds, and let $\rho_0(\mu, \sigma^2, \sigma_\alpha^2) \equiv \rho(\mu, \sigma^2, \sigma_\alpha^2|A_0)$ be the conditional prior density of the parameters specified by A_0, given that A_0 holds. Similarly let A_1 denote a hypothesis under which the broadened model holds, with the corresponding conditional density

$$\rho_1(\mu, \sigma^2, \sigma_\alpha^2, C) \equiv \rho(\mu, \sigma^2, \sigma_\alpha^2, C|A_1) \ .$$

Note that $\rho_0(\mu, \sigma^2, \sigma_\alpha^2)$ would not ordinarily be the marginal density formed from $\rho_1(\mu, \sigma^2, \sigma_\alpha^2, C)$. Now let θ_0 and $\theta_1 = 1 - \theta_0$ be the prior probabilities of A_0 and A_1, respectively, with each positive. Then it is not difficult to show, given modest assumptions concerning the two densities, that the posterior probability of A_1 goes to 1 as SSW goes to infinity. This is true no matter how small $\theta_1 > 0$ was to begin with, and thus justifies the broadening of the usual model for sufficiently extreme data. The overall posterior distribution of σ_α^2 would then be a mixture of the two conditional posterior distributions of σ_α^2, given A_0 and A_1, with most of the weight in the mixture going to A_1 when SSW is very large. On the other hand, ordinarily θ_1 will be small to begin with, and if $\hat{\sigma}_\alpha^2 > 0$ then most of the weight in the mixture will go to A_0, thus leading in effect to the usual (Bayesian) random model analysis. Now this seems to me to be the best mathematical formulation of the way in which a hypothesis is to be tested, and depending upon the data, either found wanting, found to be highly probable, or left still in doubt. It differs greatly from classical hypothesis testing, and there are no associated paradoxes, in contrast to the latter. The essential

[3] It would be more realistic to consider still other alternatives, but I shall not do so here.

idea seems to be due to Jeffreys (1961, Ch. V), although he unnecessarily requires $\theta_0 = \theta_1 = \frac{1}{2}$. Savage (1963) describes a general Bayesian approach to the testing of hypotheses.

I shall now present, without proof, a few of the results of Hill (1967). As SSW goes to infinity, the posterior probability of A_1 goes to 1, while given A_1,

$$C/\sigma^2 \xrightarrow{P} -(J-1)^{-1} ,$$

and approximately

$$\sigma^2 \sim \frac{(J-1)SSW}{J\,\chi^2_{I(J-1)}} ,$$

$$\sigma^2_\alpha \sim \frac{SSB}{J\,\chi^2_{(I-1)}} ,$$

$$\mu \sim \bar{y} + \left(\frac{MSB}{IJ}\right)^{\frac{1}{2}} t_{(I-1)} .$$

These results are in fact the results that would be obtained if there were sure prior knowledge that A_1 were true, with the correlation C/σ^2 between residuals in the same row known to take on its smallest possible value, namely $-(J-1)^{-1}$. These approximate distributions are fairly close to the exact limiting distributions, but of course differ vastly from those based upon the usual random model. Thus the data now provide substantial information about μ, σ^2_α, while they were totally uninformative about these parameters under the usual model. Finally, the overall posterior distribution of μ, σ^2, σ^2_α, can be written as the mixture of posterior densities

$$\rho_0''(\mu, \sigma^2, \sigma^2_\alpha) Pr\{A_0|\text{data}\} + \rho_1''(\mu, \sigma^2, \sigma^2_\alpha|A_1)\, Pr\{A_1|\text{data}\} .$$

As SSW goes to infinity, $Pr\{A_1|\text{data}\}$ goes to 1, and so the second term in the mixture becomes all-important. In practice how large must SSW be in order for the limiting result to be appropriate? This turns out to be a delicate matter, and can only be determined by very careful consideration of the relevant prior knowledge. This is unfortunate in that one prefers more robust inference, but I believe that any attempt to avoid consideration of such knowledge would be fatal to practice. In particular, I believe that classical significance tests which ignore such considerations are virtually worthless.

3. THE CLASSICAL APPROACH

How would a frequentist deal with a problem such as the above? I shall consider here two popular tests, namely chi-square goodness of fit and the likelihood-ratio test. In Hill (1963) I used the three-parameter log-normal model to analyze epidemic data. This model is in general use by epidemiologists and has been fit to a great variety of data. Kempthorne (1966) argued that a chi-square goodness of fit for my data gives significance at the .001 level, and used this to infer the futility of Bayesian inference. I shall ignore the fact that even the asymptotic distribution of the test statistic is unknown, so that his calculation of the significance level is quite phenomenal.[4] But even if there were significance at the 10^{-10} level I would regard this as irrelevant. For my purpose is to formulate models useful for drawing inference about those parameters I consider meaningful. I would reject the log-normal model for this purpose only if I knew of an alternative model having sufficiently high posterior probability, in much the same way as I in effect rejected A_0 in favor of A_1 for data with sufficiently large SSW. But a significant test statistic does not in itself offer any alternative model; at best it merely suggests that there may be such a model, and even here it is often misleading, since with a large sample size (mine was 310) it typically leads to rejection of the null hypothesis because of minor departures of the kind for which one does not care to reject. Such a test ignores entirely the question of whether the model is adequate for the purpose it is put to, and instead considers only whether it is the "true" model. Any sophisticated statistician knows the answer to that question even without taking data.

Not all classical tests are as foolish as the goodness of fit test. In particular the likelihood-ratio test often has some real meaning, and at least asymptotically as $SSW \to \infty$ would agree roughly with the analysis I have presented for the testing of the random model. This is because the ratio of the supremums of the likelihood function under the usual random model and under the broadened model is often approximately equal to the corresponding ratio of averaged likelihood functions, i.e.,

$$\frac{Pr\{\text{data}\,|\,A_0\}}{Pr\{\text{data}\,|\,A_1\}} = \frac{\int \cdots \int p_0(\mu, \sigma^2, \sigma_\alpha^2) Pr\{\text{data}\,|\,\mu, \sigma^2, \sigma_\alpha^2\}\, d\mu\, d\sigma^2\, d\sigma_\alpha^2}{\int \cdots \int p_1(\mu, \sigma^2, \sigma_\alpha^2, C)\, Pr\{\text{data}\,|\,\mu, \sigma^2, \sigma_\alpha^2, C\}\, d\mu\, d\sigma^2\, d\sigma_\alpha^2\, dC}.$$

[4] The sup of the likelihood function is infinite, and virtually nothing is known about even the asymptotic distribution of the relative maximum and the associated chi-square statistic.

But likelihood-ratio tests may lead to nonsensical results, of which the log-normal distribution provides a beautiful example. Thus the general meaning of such tests is obscure, and I suspect their only real justification is that they sometimes agree with posterior odds. They are also unfit to deal with the kind of delicate question mentioned at the close of section 2.

3

BAYESIAN ANALYSIS IN REGRESSION PROBLEMS

BY D. V. LINDLEY

UNIVERSITY COLLEGE LONDON

At the time of the appearance of Savage's book (1954), the Bayesian argument was not accepted seriously by more than a handful of statisticians. Now, 13 years later, a fair proportion of papers appearing in statistical journals are devoted to aspects of Bayesian theory and its application. There are several reasons for this increasing respect paid to an argument which has fluctuated in popularity during the past 200 years. First, there is the negative attitude derived from an increasing awareness of the difficulties, both theoretical and practical, in extending the orthodox, sampling theory approach to statistics beyond the stage left by Fisher and other workers of the interwar period. But second, we have the positive advantage possessed by the Bayesian approach of providing a method whereby, in principle, any statistical problem can be solved by suitable calculations involving posterior distributions: the Bayesian argument shows how a situation is to be analyzed, the orthodox methods provide no general procedure—much (perhaps too much) is left to the statistician's ingenuity. A third reason is the possibility of extending the new approach to cover situations which hardly come into the ken of the sampling theorists. Fourth, there is the justification given by Savage, De Finetti (1937) and later writers for the use of probability distributions in connection with parameters. Earlier writers, such as Jeffreys (1961) had to plead for the use of these distributions: modern work has established their existence on the basis of a few modest assumptions. And perhaps a fifth reason should be added: in most situations, Bayesian answers are identical with, or closely similar to, those we have been brought up to use. We do not have to relearn our methods.

In the present paper we discuss various features of the Bayesian approach to statistics, and, in particular, show how it can be used to elucidate some of the problems connected with the multiple regression of one variable on several other variables.

The Bayesian analysis incorporates, exactly as in the orthodox sampling[1] approach, a sample space of observations with a class of probability distributions, usually dependent on a finite number of parameters. A sample value, or observation, will be denoted by $\mathbf{x}$, and will typically be a vector, as will the parameter value $\boldsymbol{\theta}$. For given $\boldsymbol{\theta}$, the distribution, or more precisely, density of $\mathbf{x}$, will be written $p(\mathbf{x}|\boldsymbol{\theta})$; the vertical line to be read as "given." Sampling theory is concerned with finding a statistic, $t(\mathbf{x})$, which, in some sense, is near to some function $\phi(\boldsymbol{\theta})$, and can be used to estimate ϕ or test some hypothesis about it. The Bayesian argument introduces a density, $p(\boldsymbol{\theta})$, for the parameter and proceeds to use Bayes formula

$$p(\boldsymbol{\theta}|\mathbf{x}) \propto p(\mathbf{x}|\boldsymbol{\theta})p(\boldsymbol{\theta})$$

to calculate a revised density, $p(\boldsymbol{\theta}|\mathbf{x})$, for $\boldsymbol{\theta}$ given the observation $\mathbf{x}$. It is customary to call $p(\boldsymbol{\theta})$ the prior distribution, and $p(\boldsymbol{\theta}|\mathbf{x})$ the posterior distribution; but prior and posterior are really unsuitable as adjectives because they do not describe a distribution but the relation between a distribution and data. Today's posterior distribution is tomorrow's prior. But the usage is so well established we can hardly dispense with it.

Statements about $\phi(\boldsymbol{\theta})$ can be made using $p(\boldsymbol{\theta}|\mathbf{x})$, by first integrating out the unwanted aspects of $\boldsymbol{\theta}$ to find $p(\phi|\mathbf{x})$. The Bayesian equivalent of a point estimate of ϕ can then be found by taking some point description of this distribution: for example, its mean $E(\phi|\mathbf{x})$, or its mode, which latter is closely related to the maximum likelihood estimate. Interval estimates for ϕ can be found by taking intervals containing an assigned proportion of the same distributions. Hypotheses about ϕ can be tested, either by calculating the posterior probability of the null

---

[1] It is often helpful to refer to the usual statistical arguments of Fisher, Neyman, Pearson, etc., as sampling methods, because they are based on the sampling properties of statistics: properties which are not involved in many aspects of the alternative approach.

value, or by relating significance tests to interval estimates in the usual orthodox way by describing a null value as significant if it does not belong to the interval estimate, and using the Bayesian interval just mentioned. It is probably best not to follow the orthodox ideas of estimates and tests but instead to use the idea of the distribution $p(\phi|\mathbf{x})$ to provide a complete summary of the knowledge the statistician has of ϕ.

It is important to notice that the above brief description provides a method of wide generality and gives a computable procedure for making statements about ϕ. This is in contrast to the sampling approach where no equivalent procedure for deriving $t(\mathbf{x})$ is available. It is true that within the orthodox school there are recipes (for example, sufficiency) for whittling down the class of statistics: but no well-defined, general procedure exists. On the other hand, where a satisfactory orthodox technique is available, it can typically be derived, either approximately or exactly, by the Bayesian method. The special important case of normal, linear hypothesis models is one where the parallel is exact. The posterior distributions are all t, F, or χ^2 and thereby provide estimates and tests of the same practical form as the t-, F- and χ^2-tests of sampling theory. This covers the whole of the analysis of variance for model I situations, and all normal regression theory. Even when we depart from the normal distribution and discuss binomial, Poisson and related distributions, the Bayesian results are very similar to the results we are all familiar with. It is not that orthodox statistics is wrong; it is usually correct, but for the wrong reasons.

It is, of course, true that we have to pay a penalty for the ability to use Bayes' theorem. The penalty lies in the specification of the prior distribution $p(\boldsymbol{\theta})$; and it is a good and legitimate argument on the part of the orthodox school that any arbitrariness they have in the choice of statistic $t(\mathbf{x})$ is balanced by the need to select $p(\boldsymbol{\theta})$. There are two arguments against this: the first we have already had, namely it provides a general method. The second argument rests in the fact that any satisfactory solution has got to be equivalent to a Bayesian one for some prior, so why not introduce the prior openly? There are several ways this can be expressed. Wald did it by showing that, aside from a few technicalities, the class of admissible solutions, in his terminology, is exactly the Bayes class. But he used the concept of a loss function. Later writers have shown that, subject to some mild requirements, essentially that all uncertainties can be compared, any individual does possess a prior distribution: and, further, if all consequences can be compared, then any decisions should be arrived at by calculating expected utilities with respect to that distribution. To my mind the great contribution of these and similar arguments is the demonstration of the existence of distributions for parameters. That still leaves the problem of measuring them, but at least we know they are there to be measured. The analogy of length is not inappropriate: we know there exist lengths and distances, but it is still not a trivial task to measure them.[2] There remain tremendous technical difficulties in assessing prior distributions, so let us tackle them and not pretend the distributions are not there to be measured.

To my mind, these are all important reasons for using Bayes' theorem: but there remains one further reason which outweighs all the rest. It is now possible to consider, within the Bayesian framework, problems and their solutions which either did not fit comfortably, or did not appear at all, in the orthodox methods. An example is the attempt to answer the question so frequently put to a statistician: "How large a sample shall I take?" It is plainly difficult for anyone who denies the existence of a distribution for $\boldsymbol{\theta}$ to provide an answer because, before a sample is taken, the only knowledge you have is the prior knowledge whose quantification is being denied. Orthodox sampling theory was therefore unable to tackle this problem; though the ingenious solution by Grundy, Healy and Rees (1956), which is Bayesian in spirit, if not in fact, was successful and years ahead of its proper time. The determination of sample size now fits neatly into the Bayesian framework, and important results have been derived in a limited class of situations (Raiffa and Schlaifer [1961]).

Sample size determination is a particular problem within the general field of experimental design, and it is therefore natural to inquire about the possibilities of Bayesian methods being used there. In principle there is no difficulty, and one can write down the method of solution in general terms. But it is sad to have to admit that little has been done in obtaining useful solutions. I suspect that the major reason here is just simply lack of human effort. Statisticians have not looked at design problems through Bayesian spectacles. The formal procedure is known, and easily stated. The statistician has a choice amongst a number of experiments, e, of costs $c(e)$. If e were performed he would obtain a result $\mathbf{x}$ with density $p(\mathbf{x}|e, \boldsymbol{\theta})$ dependent, in the usual way, on unknown parameters, $\boldsymbol{\theta}$. After observing $\mathbf{x}$ he makes a decision $\mathbf{d}$ and incurs a loss $L(\mathbf{d}, \boldsymbol{\theta})$, if $\boldsymbol{\theta}$ is the true parameter value. In other words the approach is decision-oriented and the purpose of experimentation

[2] I understand that the distance from New York to Moscow is not known with sufficient accuracy for the most disastrous use of a missile.

is considered to be effective decision making. It is possible to look upon experimentation as designed to improve the distribution of $\boldsymbol{\theta}$; for example, by increasing its information content. This leads to a similar analysis. In passing, we repeat that the existence of costs and losses (or less negatively, of utilities) can be justified by arguments similar to those used to convince one of the need for probability distributions for parameters.

The analysis proceeds from the final stage, the loss function, back to the initial choice of e. By selecting decision $\mathbf{d}$ we incur an expected loss of

$$\int L(\mathbf{d}, \boldsymbol{\theta}) p(\boldsymbol{\theta} | \mathbf{x}, e)\, d\boldsymbol{\theta}$$

where $p(\boldsymbol{\theta}|\mathbf{x}, e)$ is the posterior distribution of $\boldsymbol{\theta}$ given $\mathbf{x}$ and e; since, at this stage we have performed e and observed $\mathbf{x}$. The decision should be chosen to minimize this expression over $\mathbf{d}$. We then have

$$\min_{\mathbf{d}} \int L(\mathbf{d}, \boldsymbol{\theta}) p(\boldsymbol{\theta} | \mathbf{x}, e)\, d\boldsymbol{\theta} ,$$

a function of $\mathbf{x}$ and e. The expected value of this over $\mathbf{x}$ for fixed e can be found; the relevant probability density being $p(\mathbf{x}|e)$, not $p(\mathbf{x}|e, \boldsymbol{\theta})$, since $\boldsymbol{\theta}$ is unknown. This is easily obtained from the equation

$$p(\mathbf{x}|e) = \int p(\mathbf{x}|\boldsymbol{\theta}, e) p(\boldsymbol{\theta})\, d\boldsymbol{\theta}$$

where $p(\boldsymbol{\theta})$ is the prior distribution of $\boldsymbol{\theta}$: that is, prior to $\mathbf{x}$ (or e). The expected value is then

$$\int \min_{\mathbf{d}} \int L(\mathbf{d}, \boldsymbol{\theta}) p(\boldsymbol{\theta} | \mathbf{x}, e)\, d\boldsymbol{\theta}\, p(\mathbf{x}|e)\, d\mathbf{x}$$

a function only of e. To this loss must be added the cost of e, and we finally solve the design problem by choosing e to minimize the total expression. That is

$$\min_{e} \int \min_{\mathbf{d}} \int L(\mathbf{d}, \boldsymbol{\theta}) p(\boldsymbol{\theta} | \mathbf{x}, e)\, d\boldsymbol{\theta}\, p(\mathbf{x}|e)\, d\mathbf{x} + c(e) .$$

Notice that the solution involves a series of alternate expectations and minimizations: the same is true of more complicated two-stage or sequential designs. Unfortunately the result of any minimization is typically an unpleasant, nonanalytic function which is difficult to handle, but the principle is quite general. A further illustration of it will be provided by the multiple regression discussion below.

In concluding this brief summary of the present situation in Bayesian statistics mention might be made of two criticisms (amongst many) that are especially worthy of attention because of the constructive element that they contain. The first criticism says that there exist in sampling theory statistics certain procedures which do not have a satisfactory counterpart in the Bayesian framework, and which the latter technique does not cover. The procedures referred to are significance tests based on the following argument: if the null hypothesis were true, the observed result, or others more extreme than it, would have very small chance of occurring, and therefore the null value is in doubt. The reason this argument has no Bayesian substitute is that it makes no open mention of alternatives to the null hypothesis; whereas the assignment of a probability distribution clearly requires specification of alternatives and their probabilities. Yet the basic, sampling argument is attractive because of its simplicity and because there are practically important situations where a well-specified null has nothing but very vague alternatives, or none at all. For example, there was a period when no reasonable alternative to Newtonian dynamics was available, and yet one felt strongly that, at best, Newtonian dynamics was only an approximation: in technical parlance, a significance test would have revealed high significance, due, among other things, to the observed advance in perihelion of Mercury. Of course, vague considerations of alternatives must come in when selecting the best criterion; but the Bayesian must admit that he cannot handle such imprecise ideas, except in limited circumstances. On the other hand the sampling solution, involving results more extreme than those observed, violates a basic Bayesian principle that argues that such results are irrelevant, and is therefore prima facie unacceptable. The situation is challenging to a Bayesian. A particular situation of the type considered in this paragraph is the "goodness-of-fit" test. Here a null hypothesis is well formulated, but the alternatives are not. Relevant references are Anscombe (1963b) and Guttman (1967).

The second criticism is related to the first because again it shows up the Bayesian's difficulty in dealing with situations precise enough for the sampling school, but too vague for him. The criticism concerns the failure of a Bayesian to escape from the parametric situation: he is unable to include nonparametric methods within his orbit. The difficulty is easily stated and is technical: no simple means exist for describing a probability distribution over the class of all probability densities on the real line. Thus we cannot express prior opinions about the distribution $p(\mathbf{x}|\boldsymbol{\theta})$ from which we are to sample unless it is restricted to a parametric class, and usually to one possessing sufficient statistics of dimensionality independent of the sample size. This leads the orthodox school to criticize the Bayesian for making assumptions that are demonstrably at best only roughly true. There may be a way out of this difficulty. A statistician loves his random sample. De Finetti has argued that it is not the random sample that is basic, but the idea of exchangeability. A sequence $X_1, X_2, \ldots, X_n$ of random variables is said to be exchangeable if the probability (or density) of any realized sequence is unaltered if that sequence is permuted in any of the $n!$ possible ways. Clearly this is true for a random sample. De Finetti's important basic theorem says that an exchangeable sequence can always be generated by taking a distribution at random (that is, according to some probability mechanism) and then taking a random sample from the selected distribution. In other words exchangeability incorporates $p(x_1|\boldsymbol{\theta})p(x_2|\boldsymbol{\theta}) \ldots p(x_n|\boldsymbol{\theta})$, the random sample, and $p(\boldsymbol{\theta})$, the distribution over the densities generating the sample. A Bayesian might find a way out of his difficulty by replacing the random sample and its troublesome distribution by an exchangeable sequence. He prefers to use the former ideas because they ensure a consistent assignment of probabilities, and consistency is his ultimate justification for all his procedures. But he might assign his probabilities by other methods that were not obviously consistent and hope to demonstrate consistency. For example, I might assign probabilities direct to the x's and not via $p(\mathbf{x}|\boldsymbol{\theta})$ and $p(\boldsymbol{\theta})$, giving $p(\mathbf{x}) = \int p(\mathbf{x}|\boldsymbol{\theta})p(\boldsymbol{\theta})\, d\boldsymbol{\theta}$. Thus, I feel that if little is known about the distribution from which a random sample has been selected, then a future observation is equally likely to lie between any two of the ordered observations in the sample. In symbols and the usual notation,

$$p(x_{(i)} < x_{(n+1)} < x_{(i+1)}|x_1, x_2, \ldots, x_n) = (n+1)^{-1}$$

with $x_{(o)} = -\infty, x_{(n+1)} = +\infty$. Is this assignment consistent? If it were it might enable one to make probability statements about the mean of the distribution, namely

$$\lim_{N \to \infty} \sum_{k=n+1}^{n+N} x_k/N ,$$

a property concerning all future observations. The assignment is probably inconsistent, but at least the idea of exchangeability might be worth pursuing.

We now turn from a rather general survey to the discussion of a particular situation, linear multiple regression, and a particular aspect of it, the use of the regression in prediction. Our aim is to demonstrate the way the Bayesian method works, and to show that it can shed new light on an old problem. The details are omitted and will be found elsewhere (Lindley [1968]). Before tackling the problem it is, however, necessary to say something about notation. The Bayesian argument centers around Bayes' theorem (hence its name) which is concerned with how the density of a single variable changes with the circumstances under which the variable is being considered: in our notation $p(\boldsymbol{\theta})$ changes to $p(\boldsymbol{\theta}|\mathbf{x})$ with the acquisition of the knowledge of $\mathbf{x}$. It follows that our notation must be rather explicit not only about the random variable, but also about the conditions. For this reason we use the vertical line, to be read "given," rather extensively. Thus $p(\boldsymbol{\theta}|\mathbf{x})$ means the density of $\boldsymbol{\theta}$ given that we know $\mathbf{x}$. Indeed, all probabilities are conditional and the notation ought always to make this clear. Consequently we shall often write $p(\boldsymbol{\theta}|H)$, where H stands for the conditions under which $\boldsymbol{\theta}$ is being considered, instead of just $p(\boldsymbol{\theta})$. The only time the vertical line will be omitted will be in the course of an argument where the conditions stay fixed throughout and it would be cumbersome to repeat them on every occasion.

When we use $p(\mathbf{x}|\mathbf{y})$ we always mean that $\mathbf{x}$ is a random variable, whose density is being referred to, and that $\mathbf{y}$ is given, fixed. Variables to the left of the line are random: those to the right are given. We shall not distinguish between a random variable $\mathbf{X}$ and the value $\mathbf{x}$ it takes. Nor shall we distinguish between densities: $p(\mathbf{x}|H)$ and $p(\mathbf{y}|H)$ are the densities of $\mathbf{x}$ and $\mathbf{y}$ given H, respectively, without any implication that these densities are the same. Similar considerations will apply to the expectation or mean. $E(\mathbf{x}|\mathbf{y})$ means the expectation of $\mathbf{x}$, given $\mathbf{y}$: the expectation operates on all quantities to the left of the vertical line for fixed, given values of those to the right. For example, $E(\mathbf{x}|\mathbf{y}, \mathbf{z})$ is a random variable function of $\mathbf{y}$ and $\mathbf{z}$, and we can calculate $E\{E(\mathbf{x}|\mathbf{y}, \mathbf{z})|\mathbf{z}\}$ which will be its expectation, given $\mathbf{z}$. It is a known result that this is equal to $E(\mathbf{x}|\mathbf{z})$.

We are concerned with a situation in which there is a single variable, y, dependent on a number, r, of independent variables $x_1, x_2, \ldots, x_r$, and we require to predict a future value of y. In view of the dependence of y on the x's it would improve the prediction if the latter could be observed and used to infer the value of y. We therefore ask the question: which of the x's is it worth observing and, having observed them, how can we best predict y? My knowledge of educational testing is slight but I imagine the following situation might occur in that field: we require to predict a person's ability y and to do this we might subject him to a number, r, of tests. Which of the tests are best suited to the assessment of his ability and, having tested him and obtained results x_i, how should we make the assessment?

To answer the question it will be necessary to have data about the tests and their relation to the ability. But we have seen above, in discussing experimental design, that the stage that comes last in time has to be analyzed first: so, for the moment, let us not consider the data in detail but simply denote by the symbol H the knowledge about y and the x's that they provide. We later return to a discussion of H. First, then, we consider the problem; given H, how to proceed.

We need a model to describe the behavior of the system and suppose the usual linear, homoscedastic regression of y on $\mathbf{x}^T = (x_1, x_2, \ldots, x_r)$:

$$E(y|\mathbf{x}, \boldsymbol{\theta}) = \boldsymbol{\theta}^T\mathbf{x} \tag{1}$$

and

$$\operatorname{var}(y|\mathbf{x}, \boldsymbol{\theta}) = \sigma^2 , \tag{2}$$

where σ^2 is a *known* constant. There $\boldsymbol{\theta}$ is the usual column vector of regression coefficients and a superfix T is used to denote transpose. It is important to notice that we shall assume that

$$p(y|\mathbf{x}, \boldsymbol{\theta}, H) = p(y|\mathbf{x}, \boldsymbol{\theta}) . \tag{3}$$

This says that we have no doubts about the model of linear regression, in the sense that the data H do not conflict in any way with it. In more usual terminology we assume a given form to the likelihood function and do not, in the present paper, discuss goodness-of-fit tests for the model.

Our problem is to observe some of the x_i and, from them, to predict y. But $\boldsymbol{\theta}$ is unknown and cannot be used in (1) for prediction, even if all the x's are observed. All we have is a distribution of $\boldsymbol{\theta}$, $p(\boldsymbol{\theta}|H)$, a distribution posterior to H. Similarly for any unobserved x_i we have a distribution and hence, overall, a distribution $p(\mathbf{x}|H)$. We shall assume these two distributions to be *independent*. The non-Bayesian will not admit either of these distributions of $\boldsymbol{\theta}$ or $\mathbf{x}$. He will have a substitute for the former in his ability to estimate $\boldsymbol{\theta}$, given H, and to provide standard errors for the estimate. The Bayesian will use the standard deviation of $\boldsymbol{\theta}$, given H, as a substitute for the latter. But the orthodox, sampling-theory statistician will usually have nothing corresponding to $p(\mathbf{x}|H)$. To him the person tested will have scores x which are constants, not random variables. To a Bayesian everything is a random variable, in the sense that he has beliefs, expressed by probabilities, concerning it. The distributions will be discussed further below.

Let us denote by I a subset of the integers $1, 2, \ldots, r$ and by J the complementary subset. A choice of I will correspond to a decision to observe x_i with $i \in I$ and not to observe those with $i \in J$. Denote the observed vector by $\mathbf{x}_I$, the unobserved by $\mathbf{x}_J$. Denote by $f(\mathbf{x}_I)$ the function of the observed $\mathbf{x}_I$ to be used to predict y. The choice of I and f corresponds to a decision about what variables to observe and how to perform the prediction. We suppose the loss in selecting I and f is given by

$$(y - f[\mathbf{x}_I])^2 + c_I \ , \tag{4}$$

where y is the true value and $c_I \geq 0$ is the cost of observing the x's with $i \in I$. It is necessary to introduce such a cost since otherwise we would observe all the x's: cost-free observations can always be expected to be valuable. Formula (4) assumes the usual quadratic loss in estimation and the addition of a cost term: though it does not assume the cost to be additive in the individual variables.

The decisions in this problem fall into two parts: first the selection of I, second the prediction using the observed x_I. Again we discuss these in reverse order. Using the standard result that squared error is least about the mean, it is trivial to show that the best predictor f is given by

$$f(\mathbf{x}_I) = E(y|\mathbf{x}_I, H) = E(\boldsymbol{\theta}|H)^T E(\mathbf{x}|\mathbf{x}_I, H) \ . \tag{5}$$

In words, estimate all the x's (for the observed this is simply $\mathbf{x}_I$, for the unobserved it is $E(\mathbf{x}_J|\mathbf{x}_I, H)$) and all the regression coefficients, using as estimates the means of the distributions, and substitute these in the regression equation (1). This is not necessarily the same as taking the linear regression of y on $\mathbf{x}_I$: indeed, it is easy to see that (5) need not be linear in the $\mathbf{x}_I$.

It is straightforward, though less trivial, to find the expected loss using I and the predictor (5). The optimum I can then be found by minimizing the resulting expression. Retaining only the relevant terms, namely those involving I (for the rest see equation [8]) we find that it is best to observe these x_i with $i \in I$, where I is chosen to satisfy

$$\min_I \{E(\boldsymbol{\theta}|H)^T V(\mathbf{x}_J|H) E(\boldsymbol{\theta}|H) + c_I\} \ . \tag{6}$$

Here $V(\mathbf{x}_J|H)$ is the dispersion matrix of the x's, given $\mathbf{x}_I$, averaged over $\mathbf{x}_I$. Given $\mathbf{x}_I$ only the variables in $\mathbf{x}_J$ have nonzero dispersions, so that all the rows and columns of $V(\mathbf{x}_J|H)$ with indices in I have zero elements, and the quadratic form in (6) involves only the $\boldsymbol{\theta}_j$ with $j \in J$.

A trivial special case may clarify the result. If the x's are independent and the costs additive in the individual variables, that is $c_I = \Sigma_{i \in I} c_i$, the expression in braces in (6) is

$$\sum_{j \in J} E(\theta_j|H)^2 \operatorname{var}(x_j|H) + \sum_{i \in I} c_i$$

and consequently x_i is observed if

$$E(\theta_i|H)^2 \operatorname{var}(x_i|H) > c_i \; . \tag{7}$$

In words, a variable is worth observing if its variation is large enough, or its corresponding estimated regression coefficient is large enough in modulus, both comparisons being made with the cost of observation. In typical situations the x's are not independent and the solution of (6) becomes substantially more difficult.

Formula (6) is interesting both for what it contains, and what it omits. Perhaps the most striking omission is any reference to the dispersions of the regression parameters, given H. As explained above, these dispersions are the Bayesian equivalent of the dispersions of the regression estimates. Consequently we are arguing that for prediction in the way we have formulated it, these errors of estimation are irrelevant. In contrast, what is relevant is the dispersion matrix of the unobserved x's: uncertainty about the value of an independent variable suggests that it would be worthwhile observing it. In other words variation in the x's is more important than in the θ's. This will influence our choice of H when we come to discuss it: since it is H that will provide $E(\boldsymbol{\theta}|H)$ and var $(\mathbf{x}_J|H)$ as the notation indicates. However, it is important to remember that the expression in braces in (6) contains only that part of the expected loss that involves I. There are other terms, specifically

$$\sigma^2 + tr\{V(\boldsymbol{\theta}|H)\,V(\mathbf{x}|H)\} + E(\mathbf{x}|H)^T V(\boldsymbol{\theta}|H) E(\mathbf{x}|H) \; , \tag{8}$$

where tr { } denotes the trace of a matrix. These do involve $V(\boldsymbol{\theta}|H)$, the Bayesian equivalent of standard errors of regression estimates, so that it is useful to have data which enable the regression to be estimated precisely. It is only in the choice of the variables to be used in the prediction that the dispersions of the regression parameter are irrelevant. The selection of optimum H will not be discussed in the present paper.

It is perhaps appropriate at this point to make some remarks about the formulation of prediction as a decision problem, and its resulting solution. We have supposed that the multiple regression relationship between y and $\mathbf{x}$ is to be used for a specific purpose, namely to predict a future value of y, and that the loss structure takes a well-defined form, given by (4). Within this framework we have asked, and found, how the prediction can best be done. In other words, we have asked a very specific question and, naturally, when you do this, you obtain a specific answer. We do not pretend that the analysis we put forward, based on (6), is appropriate for all multiple regression problems: far from it, it is put forward as a solution in some, possibly very few, cases. If the approach is narrow, what then are its advantages? To my mind its great merit lies in the fact that the formal procedure leads to a definite answer which reveals just what it is that is important and equally, what is irrelevant. This is in direct contrast to the attitude often adopted in statistics wherein one attempts to obtain insight into some data, and statistics are suggested, and ways of handling them proposed, without any explicitly stated objective being provided. Insofar as I can understand him, this is what Tukey (1962) means by data-analysis. I do not criticize this attitude: it is fine for intelligent men with sound intuition as to what is a good statistic and what is a sensible thing to do with it. But the formal procedure can usefully complement it and dispense with the intuition that most of us do not, unfortunately, possess. A crisp answer to a sharp problem is sometimes useful: equally, a fuzzy solution to a confused situation may be valuable.

Although I have said that the above approach is narrow; granted that the purpose is prediction, I do not see that there is much choice in the formulation except in regard to the loss function, (4). We need to select the variables and choose $f(.)$: we could, however, use a different loss structure. For example, we might replace quadratic loss by some other functions such as 1 if $|y - y'| > k$ and 0 if $|y - y'| \leq k$, corresponding to a desire to get within k of the true value y by the prediction y'. Obviously, we have chosen $(y - y')^2$ for reasons of mathematical simplicity. The quadratic loss concept will be familiar to statisticians, but many will be disturbed by the introduction of costs. The following arguments may make it more appealing. Suppose a situation is contemplated in which the prediction differs from the correct value by 10 units: that is $y - y' = 10$. Suppose that in that prediction, x_1, say, had not been observed. Let us consider whether to improve the prediction by using x_1 in addition to those already used. Suppose this reduced the error of prediction $y - y'$ to nine units;

would it have been worth observing x_1, bearing in mind observations always involve some effort? (In our educational example we would have had to have used an additional test.) If this answer is no, then the cost of the additional variable is greater than $10^2 - 9^2 = 19$ units. Considering other reductions in error we can bracket the cost for x_1. If, for example, the question is repeated with $y - y' = 8$ and the answer is yes, then the cost is less than $10^2 - 8^2 = 36$ units. In this way the cost can be compared with errors of prediction. I can see no way of escaping from such comparisons.

There are, of course, many uses of multiple regression outside prediction. Another possibility is where it is desired to control y at or near some target value y_o, and some, or all, of the independent variables may be controlled at selected values to assist in this control. The decisions then involve not only the selection of the variables but also the values at which these are to be held. Problems of this type have been considered by engineers; see, for example, Aoki (1967). We shall not consider such problems here (see Lindley [1968] for details) except to remark that the solution is often quite different from that derived above for the prediction problem, even in the part that is common to the two situations, namely the choice of variables to include in I. A simple illustration may illuminate the point. We saw, equation (7), that when the x's were independent and costs additive the condition for inclusion of any variable x_i for prediction purposes was very simple. A corresponding simple condition in one formulation of the control problem is to control x_i if and only if

$$E(\theta_i^2|H)\,\mathrm{var}(x_i|H) > c_i \ . \tag{9}$$

This differs from (7) only in the substitution of the expectation of the square of θ_i for the square of the expectation. In particular, the standard error of θ_i is relevant for choice of I in the control situation, but not in the prediction situation. This demonstrates how the regression analysis must depend on the requirements of the analysis.

We now turn to the consideration of H, including the data that we must use for our predictive analysis. The above result shows that all we require from H is $E(\boldsymbol{\theta}|H)$ and $\mathrm{var}(\mathbf{x}|H)$, assuming a situation in which, given H, $\boldsymbol{\theta}$ and $\mathbf{x}$ are independent. It is natural to assume that H contains at least the results of observing y and all the independent variables on a number of occasions. To be precise, suppose H contains n independent (given $\boldsymbol{\theta}$) observations $y_1, y_2, \ldots, y_n$ at values $x_{ij}(i = 1, 2, \ldots, n : j = 1, 2 \ldots, r)$, with the same density $p(y_i|\mathbf{x}_1, \boldsymbol{\theta})$ as before (and therefore satisfying [1] and [2]). Suppose further that this distribution is normal: the point being that we have to make some distributional assumption in order to use Bayes' theorem. If, in addition, we suppose that any knowledge of $\boldsymbol{\theta}$ apart from that gained from this data is slight; or, to put it another way, before observing $\mathbf{y}$ and $\mathbf{X}$, the matrix whose typical element is x_{ij}, the distribution of $\boldsymbol{\theta}$ was sensibly uniform; then it is easy to show that

$$E(\boldsymbol{\theta}|H) = (\mathbf{X}^T\mathbf{X})^{-1}\mathbf{X}^T\mathbf{y}\ , \tag{10}$$

the usual least-squares estimate of $\boldsymbol{\theta}$. (See, for example, Lindley [1965].) The identity of $E(\boldsymbol{\theta}|H)$ and $\hat{\boldsymbol{\theta}}$, the least-squares, or maximum likelihood, estimate is an example of the phenomenon we remarked on above, that the Bayesian and the sampling-theory results are often the same. Another example of this is the expression for the dispersion matrix of $\boldsymbol{\theta}$, given H, which is the same as the dispersion matrix of the least-squares estimates, namely

$$V(\boldsymbol{\theta}|H) = (\mathbf{X}^T\mathbf{X})^{-1}\sigma^2 \tag{11}$$

The distribution of $\mathbf{x}$, given H, requires more discussion, because, as explained above, it is even more alien to the sampling theorist than that of $\boldsymbol{\theta}$. Indeed, the orthodox argument would appear not to require this distribution, or even a substitute for it. It is pertinent to ask why this should be so. We shall see that what happens is that the usual argument makes a tacit assumption, that the Bayesian approach forces into the open. This, we argue, is one of the advantages of the formal, Bayesian argument; that because it involves a definite procedure, it equally involves a definite statement of assumption which the other methods, because they are less formalistic, can suppress and appear to avoid; though, in truth, they cannot.

The distribution of x is required because, if an independent variable x, is unobserved in the prediction, it needs to be estimated before it can be used in the regression equation, (5), and because the variability induced in y by this lack of observation needs to be assessed, equation (6). How are these features usually avoided? What ordinarily happens is that if only $\mathbf{x}_I$ was to be observed, the statistician would compute the *linear* regression of y on $\mathbf{x}_I$, and not on $\mathbf{x}$, from the data in H. This immediately involves one assumption, namely that the regression $E(y|\mathbf{x}_I, H)$ is linear. As we have remarked above there is no need for this to be so. However, the assumption of linearity has already been made for the full regression on $\mathbf{x}$, equation (1), and it is but a mild extension to extend the assumption to cover $\mathbf{x}_I$. But a further requirement is necessary before the reduced regression, on $\mathbf{x}_I$, can be regarded as satisfactory. It will have been estimated from H, that is, from the values $\mathbf{y}$, $\mathbf{X}$ described above and will only be sensible for prediction if, in that prediction, the unobserved x's namely $\mathbf{x}_J$, behave in the way they did in H. A simple illustration may assist the understanding. Suppose $r = 2$ and we write

$$E(y|x_1, x_2, H) = \alpha_1 x_1 + \alpha_2 x_2 \ ,$$

with $\alpha_i = E(\theta_i|H)$. Then we have

$$E(y|x_1, H) = \alpha_1 x_1 + \alpha_2 E(x_2|x_1, H) \ ,$$

and, in particular, if x_1 and x_2 are independent, given H

$$E(y|\hat{x}_1, H) = \alpha_1 x_1 + \alpha_2 E(x_2|H) \ .$$

Consider two different experiments, that is two types of H, in one of which all the values of x_2 are one unit greater than in the other. Then the regressions of y on x_1, $E(y|x_1, H)$, will also differ by unity. Both regressions cannot be correct for prediction: the correct one is the one that corresponds to the situation after H. Consequently in order to use the reduced regression we must have the same conditions in H as will occur in the prediction. This is the main tacit assumption (the other being the linearity) used in the orthodox approach: without it the method is unsatisfactory.

In the Bayesian framework these assumptions are not needed, but if they are made, in order to compare with the classical analysis, the results simplify in a way now to be explained. If it is assumed that the regression of $\mathbf{x}_J$ on $\mathbf{x}_I$ is linear (for every I), then we immediately obtain a linear regression predictor, equation (5). With this assumption $V(\mathbf{x}_J|H)$ can be rewritten in terms of $V(\mathbf{x}|H)$, the full dispersion matrix of the x's. Partitioning this latter matrix in the obvious way we may write the nonzero elements of $V(\mathbf{x}_J|H)$ in the form

$$V(\mathbf{x}_J|H) = \boldsymbol{V}_{JJ} - \boldsymbol{V}_{JI}\boldsymbol{V}_{II}^{-1}\boldsymbol{V}_{IJ} \ , \qquad (12)$$

where $\boldsymbol{V}_{II}$, etc., are the elements of the partition. The second assumption is that the independent variables in the multiple regression experiment contained in H have the same distribution as $\mathbf{x}$ in the prediction situation. If this is so then $\mathbf{x}_1, \mathbf{x}_2, \ldots, \mathbf{x}_n$ in H may be regarded as a random sample from a distribution, and $\mathbf{x}$, in the prediction, as a further sample, $\mathbf{X}_{n+1}$, from this distribution. For simplicity we assume this distribution to be multivariate normal, and hence to have the required linear regression property. We therefore require the distribution of a future observation from a multivariate normal density, given a random sample from the density. This has been found by Ando and Kaufman (1965, §2.4) and shown to be multivariate Student. We only require the mean and variance and these are

$$E(\mathbf{x}|H) = \sum_{i=1}^{n} \mathbf{x}_i/n \ , \tag{13}$$

and

$$V(\mathbf{x}|H) \sim \mathbf{W}^T\mathbf{W}/n \ , \tag{14}$$

where $\mathbf{W}$ is the matrix whose typical element is $x_{ij} - x_{\cdot j}$, $x_{\cdot j}$ denoting the mean $\sum_{i=1}^{n} x_{ij}/n$. The expression for the variance is only correct to order n. The exact result is of the form $\mathbf{W}^T\mathbf{W}n^{-1}(1 + 0(n^{-1}))$ where the term $0(n^{-1})$ does not depend on the x_{ij} but does depend on the exact form of the density of the multivariate normal dispersions prior to the multiple regression experiment in H. To simplify the argument we use (14).

It is important to realize that it is not necessary to make these assumptions about the distribution of $\mathbf{x}$. We are only doing so here in order to compare our results with those of the orthodox school wherein we argue they are tacitly made. With such assumptions we shall refer to H as containing a *random* experiment. By this we imply that the independent variables in H behaved in the same random way as they will in the prediction. There are many important practical situations where this assumption is patently false, and therefore where orthodox procedures are suspect. For example, it is common to use the multiple regression model with *designed* experiments where the x_{ij} have been fixed at selected values, chosen to have some attractive properties, such as making the estimation of the regression parameters orthogonal or increasing their precision. With such a designed experiment information about the mean and variance of $\mathbf{x}$, given H, must come from some other source than the multiple regression. We do not discuss this possibility any further, confining our attention in the rest of this paper to the random experiment.

Before proceeding, note that in a random experiment the distributions of $\boldsymbol{\theta}$ and $\mathbf{x}$ are independent as required by our earlier analysis. The reason for this is that the joint distribution of $\mathbf{y}$ and $\mathbf{x}$ is of the form

$$p(\mathbf{y}|\mathbf{x}, \boldsymbol{\theta})p(\mathbf{x}) \tag{15}$$

where the distribution of $\mathbf{x}$ does not involve $\boldsymbol{\theta}$. If, prior to H, the parameters of this latter distribution are independent of $\boldsymbol{\theta}$, then it is clear that as a result of the multiplication involved in Bayes' theorem, the same will be true posterior to H. Essentially the independence follows from the factorization of the likelihood based on (15).

With the relevant values of $E(\boldsymbol{\theta}|H)$, equation (10), and $V(\mathbf{x}|H)$, equation (14), together with the revised expression for $V(\mathbf{x}_J|H)$, equation (12), it is easy to simplify (6) and find that the optimum I must be chosen to satisfy

$$\min_I \{R(J : I)n^{-1} + c_I\} . \qquad (16)$$

There $R(J : I)$ is the reduction in sum of squares due to $\mathbf{x}_J$, given that $\mathbf{x}_I$ has already been fitted. Or, to put it another way, if we take the data from the multiple regression expression and minimize the sum of squares $\Sigma_i(y_i - \Sigma_j\theta_j x_{ij})^2$ with $\boldsymbol{\theta}_J = 0$ we obtain a residual R_I, say. If we repeat the minimization without the restriction we obtain a smaller residual R, say. Then $R(J : I) = R_I - R$, the reduction due to $\boldsymbol{\theta}_J$ or $\mathbf{x}_J$. The effective quantity to minimize is therefore $R_I + nc_I$. The optimum predictor, (5), is then the estimated linear regression of y on $\mathbf{x}_I$, in agreement with orthodox ideas. The expected loss using this predictor is

$$\sigma^2(1 + r/n) + \min_I \{R(J : I)n^{-1} + c_I\}.$$

In postulating a random experiment we have tried to provide for the orthodox analysis. Let us see how far the result agrees with suggestions put forward by sampling theorists. Most methods are based on analysis of variance ideas: for example a test of the null hypothesis that $\boldsymbol{\theta}_J = 0$ would be based on referring $R(J : I)/\sigma^2$ to χ^2 on $(r - s)$ degrees of freedom, and it might be concluded that if this test was insignificant at some preassigned significance level, then the variables $\mathbf{x}_J$ had little effect on the value of y and it would be safe to ignore them in making the prediction. Our method proceeds similarly but refers $R(J : I)/\sigma^2$ to nc_I/σ^2 and not χ^2. If the variables all have the same cost c and the costs are additive, $c_I = sc$, and the two methods are very close except for the occurrence of n, the sample size, in the Bayesian approach. The parallel could be made closer by allowing the significance level to depend on the sample size, as has been suggested elsewhere: see, for example, Lindley (1961).

The reader may at this stage be puzzled by an apparent contradiction. It has been pointed out that in general the variance of $\boldsymbol{\theta}$, given H, is irrelevant for the prediction: and yet we have finished up by almost performing a significance test for $\boldsymbol{\theta}$, which is effectively a comparison with a standard error. The explanation lies in the fact that the variances of $\boldsymbol{\theta}$ and $\mathbf{x}$ are related. To see this, compare equations (11) and (14); the matrix $\mathbf{W}$ differs from $\mathbf{X}$ only in the removal of the means in the former. This makes no effective differences since our regressions have been written in homogeneous form. Consequently $V(\boldsymbol{\theta}|H)$ apparently enters, though what is really present is $V(\mathbf{x}|H)$. Of course, this only holds for the random experiment.

Procedures more sophisticated than straight significance tests have been suggested by Newton and Spurrell (1967 a, b). They consider quantities called elements which are used to assess the merit of any x_i. It is not difficult to show that the elements are in one-to-one correspondence with the $R(J : I)$ as I runs through the 2^r possible values, and that for the case of additive constant costs the procedures are similar to ours but based on significance levels.

The most interesting suggestions that I have come across are made by Mallows (1968) (see also Gorman and Toman [1966]). One idea is called the C_p-plot technique: in our notation the C_s-plot, s being the number of variables in I. Mallows defines

$$C_s = R_I/\sigma^2 - (n - 2s) \, , \tag{17}$$

although he takes the case where σ^2 has to be estimated. If each variable has the same cost $2\sigma^2/n$, we have $c_I = 2s\sigma^2/n$ and may write

$$C_s\sigma^2 = (R_I + nc_I) - n\sigma^2 \, . \tag{18}$$

Consequently, apart from a linear transformation, C_s is equivalent to our statistic for this special cost structure. Mallows considers generalizations which, in his words, allow for "the utility of not having to consider this term x_j in future work." Like other writers he refers C_s to χ^2. (It is perhaps pertinent to repeat the challenge I have made before: if sampling theorists will tell me how their introspection arrives at a particular value for a significance test, I will explain how my prior distributions were derived. The usual honest answer is that Fisher thought of 5 percent as a suitable value of an early statistical table.) Mallows' work is also interesting because he uses weighted mean squares when the prediction is not concerned with values of $\mathbf{x}$ not used in H. Such a weight function specifies "the relative importance of the points in a region of interest." This recognizes the relevance of the random experiment, though we proceed differently by using $\text{var}(\mathbf{x}_J|H)$.

There is little that we can say about the computational procedures associated with the minimization of $R_1 + nc_I$. The obvious solution is the evaluation of R_I for all 2^r values of I. This is perfectly feasible with modern computers up to values of r about 12, $2^{12} = 4096$, but beyond that the calculation takes a considerable time. However, it may be that statisticians are too modest in their requests for computer time compared, for example, with bubble-chamber physicists or crystallographers. A method which avoids enumerating all cases has been given by Beale, Kendall and Mann (1967), though it is not clear how much saving there will be in a typical case. An elegant algorithm for enumerating all possibilities has been provided by Garside (1965). Methods that consist in adding one variable at a time are almost always unsatisfactory: for example, variable 1 may be the best single variable to include on the basis that when I contains a single element R_1 is least when $I = (1)$, but the best pair may be 2 and 3, which pair will not be considered by adding a variable to 1.

We conclude the paper with an illustration of the way in which some additional knowledge may be incorporated into the analysis. In multiple regression situations, particularly those studied in economics, it is often contended that most of the regression coefficients will be small; furthermore, one purpose of the analysis is to determine which few of the coefficients are of a reasonable magnitude, and therefore which of the independent variables have an important effect on y. This is knowledge about $\boldsymbol{\theta}$ contained in H but additional to the data already described. It may be thought of as knowledge prior to the random experiment, and as such can be incorporated into the Bayesian analysis. Suppose we express this by saying that each $\boldsymbol{\theta}_i$ is $N(0, \sigma_0^2)$, and that the $\boldsymbol{\theta}_i$ are a priori independent. This means, for example, that only about 1 in every 20 of the regression coefficients is expected to exceed $2\sigma_0$. The independence implies that knowledge of one coefficient would not affect your views about others. In formulating such a prior distribution it should be remembered what the $\boldsymbol{\theta}_i$ are, namely a measure of the effect of x_i on y when all the other x's are held fixed: they do not measure the effect of x_i on its own. Such a prior distribution has effectively been used by Stein (e.g., 1962) in his work on the estimation of the mean of the multivariate normal distribution.

H now contains both a random experiment and this additional knowledge. The posterior mean $E(\boldsymbol{\theta}|H)$ is now no longer equal to the least-squares estimate, equation (10), but is easily shown to be given by

$$E(\boldsymbol{\theta}|H) = \{\lambda\mathbf{U} + \mathbf{X}^T\mathbf{X}\}^{-1}\mathbf{X}^T\mathbf{y} \tag{19}$$

where $\lambda = \sigma^2/\sigma_0^2$ and $\mathbf{U}$ is the unit matrix of order r. It follows that the quantity to be minimized over I, equation (6), is

$$\mathbf{y}^T\mathbf{X}\{\lambda\mathbf{U} + \mathbf{X}^T\mathbf{X}\}^{-1}V(\mathbf{x}_J|H)\{\lambda\mathbf{U} + \mathbf{X}^T\mathbf{X}\}^{-1}\mathbf{X}^T\mathbf{y} + c_I\,, \tag{20}$$

with $V(\mathbf{x}_J|H)$ given by (12), where $V(\mathbf{x}|H)$ is given by (14). It does not seem possible to express this in any substantially simpler form; for example, in terms of reductions in sums of squares; but it may be computed as easily as such a reduction. The effect of (19) is to move the estimate of $\boldsymbol{\theta}$ towards the origin. The effect of (20) is to reduce the first term from its corresponding value ($\lambda = 0$) in the earlier situation and hence to reduce the chance of including a variable in the prediction.

4

DISCRIMINATORY PRACTICES[1]

BY SEYMOUR GEISSER

STATE UNIVERSITY OF NEW YORK AT BUFFALO

1. INTRODUCTION

As with most of the useful methodology of statistics, discrimination was introduced by R. A. Fisher (1936). He considered the problem of distinguishing between groups of flowers measured on p characteristics. He sought a linear combination of the p variables $x_1, \ldots, x_p$ that "best" discriminated between two groups, i.e., $\Sigma_{j=1}^{p} d_j x_j$, or in matrix notation $d'x$ where $d' = (d_1, \ldots, d_p)$ and $x' = (x_1, \ldots, x_p)$, when n_i vectors x_{ij} from group i supply a sample vector mean $\bar{x}_i$ and a sample covariance matrix $S_i = (n_i - 1)^{-1}\Sigma_j (x_{ij} - x_i)(x_{ij} - x_i)'$, $i = 1, 2$, as estimates of the population mean μ_i and a common covariance matrix Σ. Fisher then suggested that the best vector of coefficients d should be obtained by maximizing

$$[d' (\bar{x}_1 - \bar{x}_2)]^2/d'Sd \tag{1.1}$$

where $(n_1 + n_2 - 2)S = (n_1 - 1)S_1 + (n_2 - 1)S_2$. In other words, maximize the ratio of the square of a linear combination of the sample average difference between the two groups and a quantity proportional to the sample variance of that difference. The solution for d is easily obtained to be proportional to $S^{-1}(\bar{x}_1 - \bar{x}_2)$. He argued that this would

[1] This research was supported in part by NIGMS NIH Grant GM14031.

effectively separate the two groups and that utilization of the components of d could be informative in exposing the relative importance of the several variables involved in distinguishing between the two groups. If the measurements were nearly normally distributed, the sample average distance between the two groups, $(\bar{x}_1 - \bar{x}_2)'S^{-1}(\bar{x}_1 - \bar{x}_2)$ would be of value, using the normal integral transform, in assessing, the discriminatory power (or in Fisher's example "Flower Power") of the variables. If a new item z, with origin uncertain, was measured on the p characteristics, then one could use the discriminant to ascertain to which of the two groups it was closer, with the ensuing inference that it was more likely to have arisen from that group.

More generally one might ask for a method or a rule which assigns new observations most appropriately to their respective populations and find measures of the uncertainty of allocation—or to find the probability that a particular observation or set of observations belongs to one or another of the populations—or to consider which variables are most contributory to the separation of populations.

We shall attempt to discuss in this paper some of the ways the problem of discrimination may be handled. In section 2, we shall give a more formal setup of the problem, and in the third section we shall discuss the sampling-theory approach, a full treatment of which was recently given by Hills (1966) and to a lesser extent by John (1961), the latter especially for the multivariate normal case. The next two sections will discuss alternative Bayesian approaches to the problem, summarizing some of the work of the author [Geisser (1964, 1966, 1967)]. The sixth section applies the various methodologies to the multivariate normal case.

2. THE SETUP

Suppose the population Π_i, $i = 1, 2$ is specified by a continuous or discrete density $f(\cdot\,|\theta_i, \psi_i)$ with corresponding distribution function $F(\cdot\,|\theta_i, \psi_i)$ where θ_i is the set of distinct and possibly unknown parameters of Π_i, ψ_i is the set of distinct known parameters of Π_i. Let X_i be data obtained on Π_i based on n_i independent vectorial observations of dimension p. Moreover let z be a new or future vector observation to be assigned or classified or about which an inference is to be made given that it has prior probability $q_1 > 0$, of belonging to Π_i where $q_1 + q_2 = 1$. We shall assume throughout the following that q_i is known. Further let $\theta = \theta_1 \cup \theta_2$, $\psi = \psi_1 \cup \psi_2$, i.e., the total set of distinct possibly unknown and known parameters. The standard procedure is to obtain some function of z which best discriminates between the populations Π_1 and Π_2. Since the ratio of the prior probabilities times the ratio of the likelihoods is

$$q_1 f(z|\theta_1, \psi_1)/q_2 f(z|\theta_2, \psi_2) \ , \tag{2.1}$$

the function

$$U = U(z, \theta, \psi) = \log[f(z|\theta_1, \psi_1)/f(z|\theta_2, \psi_2)] \tag{2.2}$$

is used as the discriminant. Therefore for $r = q_2/q_1$, the rule is

$$\begin{aligned} U &> \log r \text{ assigns } z \text{ to } \Pi_1 \\ U &< \log r \text{ assigns } z \text{ to } \Pi_2 \ . \end{aligned} \tag{2.3}$$

(Now we have tacitly assumed that $Pr[U = \log r] = 0$ which will certainly be true if U has a continuous density; however there may be situations when $Pr[U = \log r] > 0$, e.g., possibly when $f(\cdot \mid \cdot)$ is a discrete density. Such cases are handled by either nonassignment, an arbitrary assignment, or the toss of an unbiased coin. To simplify the exposition we shall not consider this case and assume $Pr[U = \log r] = 0$.) Now we note that (2.1) is the posterior odds ratio, whence the posterior probability that $z \epsilon \Pi_i$ is

$$Pr[z \epsilon \Pi_i] = q_i f(z|\theta_i, \psi_i)/[q_1 f(z|\theta_1, \psi_1) + q_2 f(z|\theta_2, \psi_2)] \ , \tag{2.4}$$

an informative response to the question, "To which population does a particular observed z belong?", given q_1, q_2 and the relevant information concerning $f(\cdot \mid \cdot)$. Quite often one is interested in more than just assignment of the observation but more generally in how well we have done with a series of, say, n observations z_j, $j = 1, \ldots, n$, using the rule which "chooses" the population with the higher posterior probability. Therefore if we let

$$\max_{i=1,2} Pr[z_j \epsilon \Pi_i] = p(z_j) = p_j \ , \tag{2.5}$$

then, for example, the posterior probability that all the observations are correctly assigned using the rule is $\Pi_{j=1}^n p_j$. Perhaps more to the point we may ask for the probability that no more than r out of n have been misclassified; then we find, completely calculable from the known data $z_1, \ldots, z_n$, that

$$Pr\begin{bmatrix} r \text{ or less misclassified} \\ \text{out of } n \end{bmatrix} = \sum_{s=0}^{r} \sum_{j_1, \ldots, j_n}' (1 - p_{j_1}) \cdots (1 - p_{j_s}) p_{j_{s+1}} \cdots p_{j_n} \ , \tag{2.6}$$

where $j_1, \ldots, j_n$ is a permutation of the integers $1, \ldots, n$ and Σ' is the sum over all permutations. For example if $n = 3$ and $r = 1$, then

$$Pr\left[\begin{matrix}\text{1 or less misclassified}\\ \text{out of 3}\end{matrix}\right] = p_1p_2p_3 + (1-p_1)p_2p_3 + (1-p_2)p_1p_3 + (1-p_3)p_1p_2. \tag{2.7}$$

Now these probabilities are obviously only pertinent to the observations already made and do not necessarily yield information on such questions as the discriminatory power of the variables or how well the variables separate the populations, or what the long-run frequency of incorrect assignments will be. We note that if we write

$$p(z) = \max_i Pr[z \in \Pi_i] \tag{2.8}$$

then the average value of $p(z)$

$$E[p(z)] = \int_{-\infty}^{\infty} p(z)d[q_1F(z|\theta_1, \psi_1) + q_2F(z|\theta_2, \psi_2)]$$
$$= 1 - q_1\epsilon_1(\theta) - q_2\epsilon_2(\theta) = 1 - \epsilon(\theta) , \tag{2.9}$$

where $\int p(z)\, dF(z)$ represents $\int p(z)f(z)dz$ or $\Sigma p(z)f(z)$, depending on whether $f(z)$ is continuous or discrete, and

$$\epsilon_1(\theta) = Pr[U < \log r | z \in \Pi_1, \theta, \psi] \tag{2.10}$$

the error in assigning z to Π_2 when in fact it belongs to Π_1, and

$$\epsilon_2(\theta) = Pr[U > \log r | z \in \Pi_2, \theta, \psi] \tag{2.11}$$

the error in assigning z to Π_1 when in fact it belongs to Π_2. Therefore, the total true error of an incorrect assignment, that is to say the probability that a new observation will be misclassified, is

$$\epsilon(\theta) = q_1\epsilon_1(\theta) + q_2\epsilon_2(\theta) . \tag{2.12}$$

We may also interpret this as the long-run rate of misallocations of a large number of observations. This is then in a sense a measure of the discriminatory power of the variables taking into account the prior probabilities q_1 and q_2 and has its inferential interest. Also of interest is the discriminatory power of the variables alone, i.e., when $q_1 = q_2$. The discriminatory power is important because it may serve as the yardstick in determining whether the addition of new variables or the deletion of old ones is warranted.

Unfortunately it is often the case that θ is unknown, which complicates matters because all of these calculations depend on θ.

3. THE PROPAGATION OF ERRORS

When θ is unknown, a standard practice is to estimate it from available data in the form of, say, n_1 observations known to be from Π_1 and n_2 observations known to be from Π_2. In general then it seems reasonable to estimate U by a quantity

$$V = V(z, \hat{\theta}, \psi) = \log[f(z|\hat{\theta}_1, \psi_1)/f(z|\hat{\theta}_2, \psi_2)] \tag{3.1}$$

where $\hat{\theta}(X_1, X_2)$ is the estimator of θ and X_i represents the set of n_i observations from Π_i. Further the classification rule used for U is now used for V so that

$$\begin{aligned} V &> \log r \text{ assigns } z \text{ to } \Pi_1 \\ V &< \log r \text{ assigns } z \text{ to } \Pi_2 \ . \end{aligned} \tag{3.2}$$

One may use as an estimate of the posterior probability that $z \epsilon \Pi_i$

$$\begin{aligned} Pr[z\epsilon\Pi_i] &= q_i f(z|\theta_i, \psi_i)/[q_1 f(z|\theta_1, \psi_1) + q_2 f(z|\theta_2, \psi_2)] \ , \\ \hat{P}r[z\epsilon\Pi_i] &= q_i f(z|\hat{\theta}_i, \psi_i)/[q_1 f(z|\hat{\theta}_1, \psi_1) + q_2 f(z|\hat{\theta}_2, \psi_2)] \end{aligned} \tag{3.3}$$

though it may not be easy to put limits on the error of this estimate or even ascertain its frequentist properties. Further we may want to estimate the true misclassification error $\epsilon_i(\theta)$ by $\hat{\epsilon}_i(\theta)$ but there are now other pertinent errors to calculate and estimate (for ease of notation it is convenient from this point on to omit reference to the known parameter ψ). The average value of this estimator we denote by $E\hat{\epsilon}_i(\theta) = \bar{\epsilon}_i(\theta)$ and if $\bar{\epsilon}_i(\theta) = \epsilon_i(\theta)$, then $\hat{\epsilon}_i(\theta)$ is unbiased.

From the point of view of assignment using V, the most important errors are the index errors, i.e., the errors incurred in using the particular observed sample discriminant on future observations. The index or actual errors are thus defined conditional on the observed $\hat{\theta}$ and are

$$\beta_1(\hat{\theta}, \theta) = Pr[V < \log r | z\Pi_1, \theta, \hat{\theta}] \ , \tag{3.4}$$

i.e., the probability of misclassifying an observation drawn at random from Π_1 using the particular observed discriminant which is presumably the only one available underscoring its prime importance, and similarly

$$\beta_2(\hat{\theta}, \theta) = Pr[V > \log r | z \in \Pi_2, \hat{\theta}, \theta] \ . \tag{3.5}$$

The total index misclassification error is

$$\beta(\hat{\theta}, \theta) = q_1\beta_1(\hat{\theta}, \theta) + q_2\beta_2(\hat{\theta}, \theta) \ . \tag{3.6}$$

These errors are unknown since they depend on θ, so that if we estimate them by inserting $\hat{\theta}$ for θ it is known that $\hat{\beta}(\hat{\theta}, \theta) \leq \hat{\epsilon}(\theta)$, which is not quite satisfactory since we also know that $\epsilon(\theta) \leq \beta(\hat{\theta}, \theta)$, an unappealing reversal. It would seem that $\hat{\epsilon}_i(\theta)$ is more appropriate for $\epsilon_i(\theta)$ than $\hat{\beta}_i(\hat{\theta}, \theta)$ for $\beta_i(\hat{\theta}, \theta)$, since estimation of the true error $\epsilon_i(\theta)$ may be considered within the framework of repetition of $\hat{\theta}$, while $\hat{\beta}_i(\hat{\theta}, \theta)$ is presumably an estimate for the fixed $\hat{\theta}$, but also uses $\hat{\theta}$ to estimate θ. Another estimator of $\beta_i(\hat{\theta}, \theta)$ is the empirical error of misclassification (also termed apparent error) based on applying V to the sample itself and using the fraction misclassified, say m_i/n_i. This will often lead to gross underestimates of both $\epsilon_i(\theta)$ and $\beta_i(\hat{\theta}, \theta)$.

Instead of considering $\beta_i(\hat{\theta}, \theta)$ for the fixed value of $\hat{\theta}$ we may also consider it as a random variable, a function of the random set $\hat{\theta}$, i.e., from repeated samples of size n_1 and n_2 from Π_1 and Π_2. In particular we may ask for the unconditional probability that a pair of random samples of size n_1 and n_2 will misclassify a member of Π_1 chosen at random which is

$$\bar{\beta}_1(\theta) = E\beta_1(\hat{\theta}, \theta) = Pr[V < \log r | z \epsilon \Pi_1, \theta]$$
$$= \int Pr[V < \log r | z \epsilon \Pi_1, \hat{\theta}, \theta] \, dH(\hat{\theta}|\theta) \,, \qquad (3.7)$$

and similarly

$$\bar{\beta}_2(\theta) = E\beta_2(\hat{\theta}, \theta) = Pr[V > \log r | z \epsilon \Pi_2, \theta]$$
$$= \int Pr[V > \log r | z \epsilon \Pi_2, \hat{\theta}, \theta] \, dH(\hat{\theta}|\theta) \qquad (3.8)$$

where $H(\hat{\theta}|\theta)$ represents the distribution function of $\hat{\theta}$. We also note that $\epsilon(\theta) < \bar{\beta}(\theta) = q_1\bar{\beta}_1(\theta) + q_2\bar{\beta}_2(\theta)$. $\bar{\beta}_1(\theta)$ is often estimated by $\hat{\beta}_1(\hat{\theta}, \theta)$ since it may be difficult to use $\bar{\beta}_1(\hat{\theta})$.

We may also ask for limits on $\beta_1(\hat{\theta}, \theta)$ in the form of

$$Pr[a \leq \beta_i(\hat{\theta}, \theta) \leq b] = P_i(a, b, \theta) \,,$$

i.e., the unconditional probability that a random pair of size n_1 and n_2 will incorrectly assign between proportion a and b of the population of Π_i. In particular, interest is sometimes focused on the upper limit

$$Pr[\beta_i(\hat{\theta}, \theta) \leq b] = P_i(b, \theta) \,,$$

i.e., the unconditional probability that at most a proportion b of Π_i will be misclassified. Conceptually then $P_i(a, b, \theta)$ and $P_i(b, \theta)$ may be estimated by $\hat{P}_i(a, b, \theta) = P_i(a, b, \hat{\theta})$ and $\hat{P}_i(b, \theta) = P_i(b, \hat{\theta})$, and conceivably exact confidence limits can be obtained, though it may be rather difficult to do so in practice. One further point is that though $\epsilon(\theta) < \bar{\beta}(\theta)$, the usual estimate of $\bar{\beta}(\theta)$, $\bar{\beta}(\hat{\theta})$, is such that $E\bar{\beta}(\hat{\theta}) < \epsilon(\theta)$.

For a discriminating and cogent description of the many different possible allocation error rates, their frequentist interpretations and their various estimators, the reader is referred to the commendable work of Hills (1966).

4. BAYESIFICATION OF THE STANDARD PROCEDURE

The previous problems are now regarded in terms of parametric estimation from the Bayesian standpoint. We assume that the unknown set of parameters θ have a prior density given the known values of the set ψ, $g(\theta|\psi)$ or just $g(\theta)$ (once more suppressing the set ψ for ease of notation). We may wish to obtain a Bayesian estimate of the posterior probability that $z \epsilon \Pi_i$ for fixed θ,

$$\frac{q_i f(z|\theta_i)}{q_1 f(z|\theta_1) + q_2 f(z|\theta_2)} = Pr(z \in \Pi_i|\theta) \ . \tag{4.1}$$

Consider (4.1) as a function of the set θ and therefore a random variable whose density is derivable in principle from the posterior density of θ which is

$$P(\theta|X) \propto L(X_1|\theta_1)L(X_2|\theta_2)g(\theta) \tag{4.2}$$

where $L(X_i|\theta_i)$ represents the likelihood of θ_i given the data X_i based on n_i observations from Π_i. Further we may ask for the average conditional probability (i.e., averaged over all values of θ) that $z \epsilon \Pi_i$

$$\overline{Pr}(z \in \Pi_i) = \int Pr(z \in \Pi_i|\theta) P(\theta|X) \, d\theta = EPr(z \in \Pi_i|\theta) \ , \tag{4.3}$$

and utilize this as the Bayesian estimator that minimizes the squared error loss function as an alternative for (3.3). The density of the true misclassification error $\epsilon_i(\theta)$ is also obtained from $P(\theta|X)$, and similarly the unconditional true misclassification error

$$\bar{\epsilon}_i = E\epsilon_i(\theta) = \int \epsilon_i(\theta) P(\theta|X) \, d\theta \ , \tag{4.4}$$

as a Bayesian estimator of $\epsilon_i(\theta)$.

$\beta_i(\hat{\theta}, \theta)$, via the Bayesian approach, is inherently conditioned on $\hat{\theta}$ and the unconditional index error is $\bar{\beta}_i = E\beta_i(\hat{\theta}, \theta) = \int \beta_i(\hat{\theta}, \theta) P(\theta|X) \, d\theta$, i.e., averaged over θ in contradistinction to $\bar{\beta}_i(\theta)$, which is the resultant average of the same quantity over θ. Further we may compute

$$Pr[a \leq \beta_i(\hat{\theta}, \theta) \leq b] = P_i(a, b) \ , \tag{4.5}$$

the probability that the index error is in the interval $[a, b]$ and

$$Pr[\beta_i(\hat{\theta}, \theta) \leq b] = P_i(b) \ , \tag{4.6}$$

the probability that the index error is at most b, from the posterior density of $\bar{\beta}_i(\hat{\theta}, \theta)$ where θ is the set of random variables. Since

$$\epsilon(\theta) \leq \beta(\hat{\theta}, \theta) \tag{4.7}$$

it is clear that

$$\bar{\epsilon} = E\epsilon(\theta) \leq E\beta(\hat{\theta}, \theta) = \bar{\beta} \tag{4.8}$$

and

$$Pr[\epsilon(\theta) \leq b] \geq Pr[\beta(\hat{\theta}, \theta) \leq b] \ ,$$

so that in this approach all of the inequalities are in their appropriate order.

One could also find and discuss the posterior density of $\bar{\beta}_i(\theta)$, but this error seems to be entirely irrelevant even from this Bayesian standpoint.

5. THE "COMPLEAT" BAYESIAN

The frequentist approach is based on the sampling distributions of the quantities

$$U = \log \frac{f(z|\theta_1, \psi_1)}{f(z|\theta_2, \psi_2)}$$

and

$$V = \log \frac{f(z|\hat{\theta}_1, \psi_1)}{f(z|\hat{\theta}_2, \psi_2)} \ .$$

The Bayesification of this approach essentially involves making inferences concerning the discriminatory power of the variables from the posterior densities of these and other associated quantities. We now discuss another approach which is completely Bayesian in that it concerns itself with odds ratios of the predictive densities of future observations,

$$W = \log \frac{f(z|X, \psi_1, \Pi_1)}{f(z|X, \psi_2, \Pi_2)} , \tag{5.1}$$

where (suppressing ψ)

$$f(z|X, \Pi_i) = \int f(z|\theta_i) P(\theta|X) \, d\theta \, . \tag{5.2}$$

The assignment of z to Π_1 may be made whenever $W > \log r$ and to Π_2 when $W < \log r$. In fact here we have a single number for the predictive probability that $z \epsilon \Pi_i$ a posteriori

$$Pr(z \epsilon \Pi_i) = q_i f(z|X, \Pi_i) / [q_1 f(z|X, \Pi_1) + q_2 f(z|X, \Pi_2)] , \tag{5.3}$$

which in regard to an inference about an observed z evidently yields all that is necessary. The discriminatory power of the variables for this approach is defined in terms of the predictive densities. Let β_i represent the predictive probability that z has been classified as belonging to Π_j, when in fact it belongs to Π_i, then

$$\beta_i = \int_{R_j} dF(z|X, \Pi_i) \tag{5.4}$$

where R_j represents the set of values of z for which

$$q_i f(z|X, \Pi_i) < q_j f(z|X, \Pi_j) \, . \tag{5.5}$$

Therefore the total predictive misclassification probability is

$$\beta = q_1 \beta_1 + q_2 \beta_2 = q_1 \int_{R_2} dF(z|X, \Pi_1) + q_2 \int_{R_1} dF(z|X, \Pi_2) \, . \tag{5.6}$$

In general then for this approach (5.3) and (5.4), (5.6) are the relevant entities for the future observation and the power of the index discriminant.

This approach can be further generalized to the classification of observations $z_1, \ldots, z_n$ that for one reason or another need be classified sequentially, and when z_n is to be classified information relevant to $z_1, \ldots, z_{n-1}$ is taken into account. Another alternative is to jointly classify $z_1, z_2, \ldots, z_n$. Both these alternatives are considered in detail in Geisser (1966). This involves one important difference from the case where θ is known, and that is the joint predictive density of future observations $z_1, z_2, \ldots, z_n$ is such that in general they are dependent, in contradistinction to their being independent when θ is known.

6. THE MULTIVARIATE NORMAL CASE

Suppose that Π_i is specified by a multivariate normal density $N(\mu_i, \Sigma)$ $i = 1,2$, so that the two populations under consideration have the same covariance structure. In this case the population and sample discriminants turn out to be linear;

$$U = [z - \tfrac{1}{2}(\mu_1 + \mu_2]'\Sigma^{-1}(\mu_1 - \mu_2) \tag{6.1}$$

$$V = [z - \tfrac{1}{2}(\bar{x}_1 + \bar{x}_2)]'S^{-1}(\bar{x}_1 - \bar{x}_2) \tag{6.2}$$

where $\bar{x}_i$ is the sample mean based on n_i observations and S is the usual unbiased sample covariance matrix based on $\nu = n_1 + n_2 - 2$ degrees of freedom. Now it is easily shown that

$$\epsilon_1(\theta) = Pr[U < \log r | \mu_1, \mu_2, \Sigma^{-1}, z\epsilon\Pi_1] = \Phi\left(\frac{\log r - \frac{1}{2}\alpha}{\alpha^{\frac{1}{2}}}\right) \tag{6.3}$$

$$\epsilon_2(\theta) = Pr[U > \log r | \mu_1, \mu_2, \Sigma^{-1}, z\epsilon\Pi_2] = 1 - \Phi\left(\frac{\log r + \frac{1}{2}\alpha}{\alpha^{\frac{1}{2}}}\right) \tag{6.4}$$

where Φ is the standardized normal distribution function and

$$\alpha = (\mu_1 - \mu_2)'\Sigma^{-1}(\mu_1 - \mu_2) \tag{6.5}$$

The estimators of $\epsilon_1(\theta)$ and $\epsilon_2(\theta)$ may be taken to be

$$\Phi\left(\frac{\log r - \frac{1}{2}Q}{Q^{\frac{1}{2}}}\right) \tag{6.6}$$

$$1 - \Phi\left(\frac{\log r + \frac{1}{2}Q}{Q^{\frac{1}{2}}}\right) \tag{6.7}$$

respectively where

$$Q = (\bar{x}_1 - \bar{x}_2)'S^{-1}(\bar{x}_1 - \bar{x}_2)\ . \tag{6.8}$$

Confidence limits on $\epsilon_i(\theta)$ may be obtained depending on confidence limits on α through the sampling distribution of cQ which is $\nu p(\nu - p - 1)^{-1}F(p, \nu - p - 1)$ where F is noncentral F with non-centrality parameter $c\alpha$ where $c = n_1 n_2\ (n_1 + n_2)^{-1}$. For details see [4]. The index or actual errors are found to be

$$\beta_1(\hat{\theta}, \theta) = Pr[V < \log r | \hat{\theta}, \theta, z\epsilon\Pi_1]$$
$$= \Phi\left[\frac{\log r + [\frac{1}{2}(\bar{x}_1 + \bar{x}_2) - \mu_1]'S^{-1}(\bar{x}_1 - \bar{x}_2)}{[(\bar{x}_1 - \bar{x}_2)'S^{-1}\Sigma S^{-1}(\bar{x}_1 - \bar{x}_2)]^{\frac{1}{2}}}\right] \tag{6.9}$$

$$\beta_2(\hat{\theta}, \theta) = Pr[V > \log r | \hat{\theta}, \theta, z \epsilon \Pi_2]$$

$$1 - \Phi\left[\frac{\log r + [\frac{1}{2}(\bar{x}_1 + \bar{x}_2) - \mu_2]' S^{-1}(\bar{x}_1 - \bar{x}_2)}{[(\bar{x}_1 - \bar{x}_2)' S^{-1} \Sigma S^{-1}(\bar{x}_1 - \bar{x}_2)]^{\frac{1}{2}}}\right] \tag{6.10}$$

and we notice that using the usual estimates that

$$\hat{\beta}_1(\hat{\theta}, \theta) = \Phi\left(\frac{\log r - \frac{1}{2}Q}{Q^{\frac{1}{2}}}\right) \tag{6.11}$$

$$\hat{\beta}_2(\hat{\theta}, \theta) = 1 - \Phi\left(\frac{\log r + \frac{1}{2}Q}{Q^{\frac{1}{2}}}\right) \tag{6.12}$$

which are identical to the estimators for $\epsilon_1(\theta)$ and $\epsilon_2(\theta)$. The unconditional index errors or the mean actual errors computed over the joint sampling density of $\bar{x}_1$ $\bar{x}_2$ and S,

$$E\beta_1(\hat{\theta}, \theta) = \bar{\beta}_1(\theta) = Pr[V < \log r | \theta, z \in \Pi_1] \tag{6.13}$$

$$E\beta_2(\hat{\theta}, \theta) = \bar{\beta}_2(\theta) = Pr[V > \log r | \theta, z \in \Pi_2] \tag{6.14}$$

are rather difficult to obtain explicitly, although approximations have been obtained by Okamoto (1963). Similarly approximations are available for $P_i(b, \theta)$. For example when $q_1 = q_2$, the following estimates (see Hills, 1966) are given for

$$\hat{\epsilon}_1(\theta) = \hat{\beta}_1(\hat{\theta}, \theta) = \Phi(-\tfrac{1}{2}Q^{\frac{1}{2}}) \tag{6.15}$$

$$P_1(b, \theta) = Pr[\beta_1(\hat{\theta}, \theta) \leq b] \cong \Phi[2c^{\frac{1}{2}}(\Phi^{-1}(b) + \tfrac{1}{2}\alpha^{\frac{1}{2}})] \tag{6.16}$$

with estimator $\hat{P}_1(b, \theta)$ given by inserting Q for α above.

The semi-Bayesian approach has been worked out by Geisser (1964) using as prior density for $\mu_1, \mu_2, \Sigma^{-1}, g(\mu_1, \mu_2, \Sigma^{-1}) \propto |\Sigma|^{(p+1)/2}$. In this approach the quantity $\epsilon_i(\theta)$ turns out to be a function of the random variable α where the posterior distribution of $c\alpha$ has density

$$\sum_{j=0}^{\infty} w_j f(c\alpha | p + 2j) \tag{6.17}$$

where $f(\cdot | p + 2j)$ is the density of χ^2 with $p + 2j$ degrees of freedom and

$$w_j = \left(\frac{\nu}{\nu + cQ}\right)^{\nu/2} \left(\frac{cQ}{\nu + cQ}\right)^j \binom{(\nu/2) + j - 1}{j}.$$

The details of the use of (6.17) for putting limits on $\epsilon_i(\theta)$ are worked out in [5] with a similar treatment for $\beta_i(\hat{\theta}, \theta)$. At any rate for $q_1 = q_2$

one finds that the unconditional true error or the mean of the posterior distribution of $\epsilon_1(\theta)$, utilizing a normal approximation for U, is

$$\bar{\epsilon}_1 = Pr[U < 0 | z\epsilon\pi_1] \cong \Phi[-\tfrac{1}{2}(pc^{-1} + Q)/(pc^{-1} + Q + c^{-1}Q)^{\frac{1}{2}}] \quad (6.18)$$

and the unconditional index error or the mean of the posterior density of $\beta_1(\hat{\theta}, \theta)$ is

$$\begin{aligned}\bar{\beta}_1 &= E\beta_1(\hat{\theta}, \theta) = Pr[V < 0 | z\epsilon\Pi_1] \\ &= Pr\left[t_{\nu+1-p} < -\frac{1}{2}\left(\frac{Qn_1(\nu - p + 1)}{(n_1 + 1)\nu}\right)^{\frac{1}{2}}\right] \quad (6.19)\end{aligned}$$

where $t_{\nu+1-p}$ is Student's t with $\nu + 1 - p$ degrees of freedom. In fact it would be of some interest to investigate $\bar{\beta}_1$ as a frequentist estimator of $\beta_1(\hat{\theta}, \theta)$, i.e., as an alternative to $\Phi(-\frac{1}{2}Q^{\frac{1}{2}})$ or some of the other proposed sampling estimators of $\beta_1(\hat{\theta}, \theta)$. Further we can obtain

$$Pr[\epsilon_1(\theta) \le b] \cong 1 - F_d\left[\frac{4c(p + cQ)}{p + cQ + \nu^{-1}(cQ)^2}(\Phi^{-1}(b))^2\right] \quad (6.20)$$

where $F_d(\cdot)$ is the distribution function of χ^2 with $d = (p + cQ)^2/(p + cQ + (cQ)^2\nu^{-1})$ degrees of freedom. Moreover it can be shown from Geisser (1967) that

$$Pr[\beta_1(\hat{\theta}, \theta) \le b] \cong \Phi\left[\frac{\Phi^{-1}(b) + \frac{1}{2}[(\nu - p + \frac{1}{2}/\nu)Q]^{\frac{1}{2}}}{(n_1^{-1} + (8\nu)^{-1}Q)^{\frac{1}{2}}}\right] \quad (6.21)$$

In the complete Bayesian approach the discriminant

$$W = \log\frac{f(z|X, \Pi_1)}{f(z|X, \Pi_2)} \quad (6.22)$$

is

$$\begin{aligned}W &= \frac{p}{2}\log\frac{n_1}{n_2} + \frac{v + 1 - p}{2}\log\frac{n_1 + 1}{n_2 + 1} \\ &\quad + \frac{\nu + 1}{2}\log\left[\frac{(n_2 + 1)\nu + n_2(\bar{x}_2 - z)'S^{-1}(\bar{x}_2 - z)}{(n_1 + 1)\nu + n_1(\bar{x}_1 - z)'S^{-1}(\bar{x}_1 - z)}\right] \quad (6.23)\end{aligned}$$

and the posterior probability that $z\epsilon\Pi_1$ is

$$Pr[z\epsilon\Pi_1] = \frac{q_1e^W}{q_2 + q_1e^W} \quad (6.24)$$

The predictive error of misclassification β_1 is to be calculated for those regions for which $q_1 f(z|X, \Pi_1) < q_2 f(z|X, \Pi_2)$ over the density of $f(z|X, \Pi_1)$, with a similar definition for β_2. The number of regions clearly depends on the number of intersections of the two predictive densities. In the case $q_1 = q_2$ and $n_1 = n_2$ there is but one intersection and the discriminant can be transformed into V, resulting in the predictive error of misclassification β_1 being identical to the mean error $\bar{\beta}_i$ of the semi-Bayesian approach. If one or both of the conditions $n_1 = n_2$, $q_1 = q_2$ do not obtain, the natural linearity manifest in both the frequentist and semi-Bayesian approach is no longer preserved. On the other hand if we are dealing with the case of unequal covariance matrices, there is no difficulty in obtaining a complete Bayesian solution, Geisser (1964), but the problem seems fairly formidable for the former approaches.

We may illustrate by a numerical example various estimates obtained from some data extracted from Fisher (1936), with regard to a taxonomic problem involving 50 observations from each population, Iris versicolor Π_1 and Iris setosa Π_2. The data are given in centimeters for four variables of which we shall only utilize for illustrative purposes the first two, x_{1i} = sepal length, x_{2i} = sepal width. In summary we have

$$\bar{x}_1 = \begin{pmatrix} 5.936 \\ 2.770 \end{pmatrix}; \qquad \bar{x}_2 = \begin{pmatrix} 5.006 \\ 3.428 \end{pmatrix}; \qquad S = \frac{1}{98}\begin{pmatrix} 19.1434 & 9.0356 \\ 9.0356 & 11.8658 \end{pmatrix}$$

Hence $n_1 = n_2 = 50$, $\nu = 98$, $p = 2$, $c = 25$, $Q = 19.94$. Assuming that $q_1 = q_2$, then from the sampling point of view

$$\hat{\epsilon}_1(\theta) = \hat{\beta}_1(\hat{\theta}, \theta) = \Phi(-2.233) = .013$$

$$\hat{P}_1(.02, \theta) = \hat{P}r[\beta_1(\hat{\theta}, \theta) \leq \cdot\, 02] \cong \Phi[10(\Phi^{-1}(.02) + 2.33)] = .96$$

From the semi-Bayesian approach we obtain

$$\bar{\epsilon}_1 \cong \Phi[-2.192] = .016$$

$$\bar{\beta}_1 = Pr[t_{97} < -2.199] \cong .016$$

$$P_1(.02) = Pr[\beta_1(\hat{\theta}, \theta) < .02] \cong .79\,.$$

We also note if $n_1 = n_2 = 10$, but Q unchanged, that while the frequentist estimates are unaltered except for $\hat{P}_1$ $(.02, \theta)$ (where the approximation is probably too poor to use),

$$\bar{\epsilon}_1 \cong \Phi(-2.062) = .020,$$

$$\bar{\beta}_1 = Pr[t_{17} < -2.069] = .027,$$

and

$$Pr[\beta_1(\hat{\theta}, \theta) < .02] \cong \Phi(.17) = .57 .$$

For $n_1 = n_2 = 5$ and the same value of Q, we report the calculation for $\bar{\epsilon}_1$ but its accuracy is subject to question,

$$\bar{\epsilon}_1 \cong \Phi(-1.930) = .027$$

$$\bar{\beta}_1 = Pr[t_7 < -1.907] = .047 .$$

The largest value that $\bar{\beta}_1$ attains for the fixed Q is when $n_1 = n_2 = 2$

$$\bar{\beta}_1 = Pr[t_1 < -1.289] = .209 .$$

It is clear that for $q_1 = q_2$, n_2 and Q arbitrary but fixed that $\bar{\beta}_1$ takes on its maximum at $n_1 = 2$, which is

$$Pr\left[t_{n_2+1-p} < -\frac{1}{2}\left[\frac{2Q(n_2+1-p)}{3n_2}\right]^{\frac{1}{2}}\right] \tag{6.25}$$

and decreases monotonically as $n_1 \to \infty$ to a minimum at

$$\Phi(-\tfrac{1}{2}Q^{\frac{1}{2}}), \tag{6.26}$$

which is entirely sensible.

The symptotic value for $\bar{\epsilon}_1$ is also (6.18).

It is clear then that both $\bar{\epsilon}_i$ and $\bar{\beta}_i$ are important; the first yields essentially the potential misclassification error while the second gives the error incurred in using the actual discriminant in hand. Obviously then if $\bar{\beta}_i$ is too large for one's purposes but $\bar{\epsilon}_i$ looks promising, then one should get more data from Π_1 and Π_2 to try and drive $\bar{\beta}_i$ down to the range of $\bar{\epsilon}_i$. If on the other hand $\bar{\epsilon}_i$ is also too large one might want to obtain measurements on variables other than just the original p in order to diminish $\bar{\epsilon}_i$ and $\bar{\beta}_i$. However when the discriminant is actually being used for allocation purposes it is $\bar{\beta}_i$ which is informative.

5

SOME COMMENTS ON BAYESIAN METHODS

BY C. L. MALLOWS

BELL TELEPHONE LABORATORIES, INCORPORATED

1. INTRODUCTION

I believe that my participation in this symposium was invited in an attempt to provide some counterweight (not to say opposition) to the other speakers. It is perhaps an interesting commentary on recent developments in statistical theory that when I considered how best to present my misgivings concerning the Bayesian approach, I felt myself to be very much on the defensive. Certainly, in view of the impressive qualifications of the other participants, and taking note of the flood of Bayesian papers that is now appearing in the statistical literature, a critic would do well to choose his stance with the utmost care. On the other hand, the ensuing discussion is likely to be more productive (certainly more lively) if fairly extreme points of view are presented. Let me make it clear at the outset that I am not committed to, nor an advocate for, any one philosophy—certainly I do not wish to defend "classical" methods as against "Bayesian" ones—rather my position is that I think that both attitudes are valuable, even essential, while neither provides an adequately complete theory of inference. I explain my position more fully below in a discussion of some aspects of the study by Mosteller and Wallace (1964), of the authorship of the Federalist papers. I shall also describe two areas of research in Bayesian methodology that seem to warrant further investigation.

2. SIMILARITIES BETWEEN BAYESIAN AND FREQUENTIST THEORIES

From reading the literature one might suppose that a major part of the effort in executing a typical Bayesian analysis is devoted to computing likelihoods and hence posterior probabilities. I would regard this activity as an exercise in probability theory, similar in kind to the maneuvers required to set up a Neyman–Pearson test. The mere use of Bayes' theorem is not a defining event! Even frequentists use conditional probability.

On the other hand, the claim is made that these calculations result in quantities that can be interpreted directly, that is, without any further reference to the data or the model used. Again, this is similar in kind to the corresponding claim in the strict Neyman–Pearson theory; once the decision has been made, a priori, to use a hypothesis test or confidence interval estimate, then the outcome of the procedure is an equivocal directive for future belief (or for action "as if"). Thus each of these two theories claims to be a theory of inference, in the sense that once the decision has been made to accept the theory, and the data becomes available, then the analyst has nothing to do but to turn the handle and accept the product, be it a decision or a statement of likelihoods or proper posterior beliefs.

3. INFORMAL METHODS: THE SELECTION EFFECT

Let me be the first to agree that the above is a grossly distorted description of how either a classical or a Bayesian analysis would actually proceed. In practice, except possibly in the routine application of a quality control procedure, few would recommend that a decision procedure should be applied strictly according to the book. I hope the same is true regarding Bayesian methods. One has to use formal theory in an informal way. For example, a methodological tool of enormous value is the device of plotting the residuals from some fitted model against the values of some variable, which may be one that enters into the model being fitted, or alternatively that may not have entered into the analysis previously. It often occurs that after examining several such plots, one will be found that suggests a way in which the fitted model is systematically inadequate. Once the peculiarity has been noticed, it is usually easy to construct a quantitative measure of the strength of the indication. For a specific example, if a plot of residuals $y_i - \hat{y}_i$ against fitted values $\hat{y}_i$ suggests that the residual variance may be increasing linearly with y, one might compute a least-squares regression coefficient b of $(y_i - \hat{y}_i)^2$ on $\hat{y}_i$. I think it is accurate to say that a tentative, exploratory analysis such as this cannot be fitted into any known formal system of inference. A frequentist might compare the computed value of b with a null-hypothesis reference distribution (possibly generated by Monte Carlo simulation), but will then have to discount the resulting tail-area probability in some way to allow for the selection effect. A Bayesian would construct a model containing a new parameter β, a population analog of b, and would compute the likelihood function of all the parameters, including β;[1] he might then wish to integrate out β or all except β. However, the Bayesian meets exactly the same difficulty as the frequentist. Before seeing the data, the parameter β was not considered at all; it has been introduced only because the data suggested it. It seems to be logically impossible to have an honest subjective prior distribution for a parameter of whose very existence one is unaware. Some would advocate the use of an arbitrary rule (such as Bayes' or Jeffreys') in situations such as this; it is not clear to me that this will make proper allowance for the selection effect, and I cannot imagine how empirical evidence could be collected to justify the use of one rule rather than another.

4. MODEL BUILDING: THE FEDERALIST STUDY

It is instructive to consider how the authors of the monumental study on the authorship of the disputed Federalist papers[2] proceeded in their construction and use of a statistical model, since they were able to avoid this selection effect in a particularly satisfying way. However, we shall find that our discussion will lead us to consider some further difficulties that arise in a formal Bayesian analysis.

In a sense, this was a particularly straightforward problem, since the data available were fairly homogeneous, and not too large to be completely unwieldy, while the general outline of the analysis could be formulated fairly confidently at an early stage. (I do not intend in any way to detract from the enormous ingenuity and uncommon application that is clearly evident in every phase of Mosteller and

[1] Likelihood functions are much harder to estimate by Monte Carlo than are null-hypothesis tail areas.

[2] All subsequent references to this study refer to Mosteller and Wallace (1964); see also Mosteller and Wallace (1963).

Wallace's analysis. The appearance of their book is truly a landmark—and a benchmark—for the statistical profession.)

In Chapter 2, Mosteller and Wallace concentrated on a finite population (not completely well defined, but containing no more than a few hundred elements) of noncontextual words of medium to high frequency. They had available finite populations (a few hundred elements for each author in dispute) of blocks of text of known authorship (by Hamilton and by Madison). Each block was of roughly the same length, 200 words.

Study of the rates of occurrence for a subset of words of this type (not a random sample) showed that some of these rates exhibited the sort of variability that is described by the Poisson model; others were more variable, and for these a negative binomial model seemed to provide better fits.[3] The whole of the rest of the "main study" was based on the negative binomial assumption (which contains the Poisson as a special case). For simplicity of exposition, let us pretend that the Poisson model had been found to be adequate throughout. The numerical differences are "huge," but the additional complexity of the negative binomial analysis raises no new points of principle.

For each word, Mosteller and Wallace postulated two parameters μ_H, μ_M governing the mean rates of occurrence of that word in passages of standard length by the two authors in dispute, Hamilton and Madison. They defined

$$\sigma = \mu_H + \mu_M, \qquad \tau = \mu_H/(\mu_H + \mu_M)$$

so that σ measures average rate of occurrence, while τ is a measure of discriminatory power.

In section 3.2, a further model-building step was made. A study of the rates of use by the two authors of each of a set of 90 words, unselected for ability to discriminate and representative of the pools of words from which all words were selected, exhibited a distribution of values of (estimates of) σ and τ such that for each value of σ, τ was distributed symmetrically about $\tau = \frac{1}{2}$. The analysts chose to represent this conditional distribution of τ as being Beta with parameters 10, 10.[4] The choice of distribution of σ is comparatively irrelevant,

[3] I think it a weakness in the study that the authors were content to assess the goodness of fit of the two models by direct comparisons of observed and expected frequencies, without computing χ^2 statistics.

[4] Several alternative choices were explored; the final results were not affected greatly.

since the data is much stronger in this direction. A locally uniform distribution was assumed.

Now comes a key assumption. Mosteller and Wallace assumed that the set of words that they proposed to use in discriminating between Hamilton and Madison could be regarded as a random sample from a population described by the above Uniform-Beta distribution. Once this step is made, the rest of the analysis follows fairly mechanically (though not without much effort and ingenuity). Using the observed counts on passages of known authorship, posterior distributions of the (σ, τ) pairs for each of the words used can be obtained; then using the counts for a disputed paper and integrating out the (σ, τ) parameters[5] an odds ratio for Hamilton versus Madison results. In the event, Madison is strongly favored, for each of the 12 disputed papers.

The set of words used in this final calculation was chosen after careful study of their discriminatory power in passages of known authorship; but, as Mosteller and Wallace remark (section 3.3),

> allowance for selection and regression effects is made entirely through the prior distributions of σ and τ. We assume that the prior distributions apply to any and every word chosen from some large pool of words. Then, according to the model, the prior distribution will reduce the apparent discriminating power to the required extent. With this selection feature, we may choose words for inclusion by whatever methods are convenient, so long as they are independent of the unknown papers.

The argument is unexceptionable, once the key assumption is made. Mosteller and Wallace are able to present[6] some empirical evidence to support the view that selection effects have been properly allowed for.

5. COMMENTS ON THE MODEL AND ITS CONSTRUCTION

Let us consider the sorts of assumption that are involved here. Notice that there is a finite population of relevant words, and a finite population of relevant text of known authorship. The analysts are in the position of having enumerated a substantial fraction of the whole of the relevant data. If they had been even more industrious than they were in fact, they might have studied effectively all the suitable words

[5] Actually Mosteller and Wallace used approximate methods based on the mode of the posterior distribution of (σ, τ). Their study of this approximation is only one of several substantial technical investigations reported.

[6] In an informal way.

on all the relevant texts. What then would be the role of the Poisson[7]-Uniform-Beta model? We are not concerned with trying to infer some psychological truth regarding the way an author's mind works in composing a passage of text. We are not concerned with guessing how data for other authors, or for these authors at other times, might behave.[8]

I suggest that it is proper to view the model as simply a way of graduating the data, in a way completely analogous to that in which a Euclidean straight line can be an approximate representation of a piece of string. *No probability concept is involved in this interpretation of the model.* Of course, one way of expressing what the model *is* (rather than how it relates to the inference problem) is to say that for any one of the words studied, if a passage of Madison text were to be chosen at random (i.e., uniformly from amongst all that are available), then in repeated trials the frequency of use of that word would exhibit (approximately) Poisson variation, and similarly for Hamilton. Further, if a word were to be chosen at random (from the population studied), then in repeated trials its differential rate of use (as between the two authors, over all the available text) would exhibit (approximately) Beta variation. However, this says nothing about how the model is to be used in relation to the 12 papers of disputed authorship.

Let me make some points at this stage, with respect to this particular study. I think they are indicative of general principles.

First, in my view there is nothing particularly Bayesian or classical or even probabilistic about the model that has been fitted to the empirical data.

Second, the problem of choosing the *form* of the model involves ill-defined concepts of relevance and symmetry, and other concepts of how observations behave in situations judged to be analogous to the one under study; thus in this case the fact that the Poisson distribution can arise from the operation of a Poisson process, and the recognition that a negative binomial distribution can be a mixture of Poissons, are reasons for considering these distributional shapes. There is little similar support for the Beta assumption, but this is mathematically convenient, and as it turns out this choice is not crucial anyway.

---

[7] Or negative binomial.

[8] Mosteller and Wallace assert (section 3.2A) that "for [pairs of] authors writing together on the same topic at the same period, we suppose that the prior distribution of τ for any word would be [adequately represented by a symmetric Beta distribution]." However, this seems to claim unnecessarily wide applicability of the model. Empirical validation of this assumption would require study of how various pairs of authors did in fact differ in their use of various words.

Except for the possibility of a theoretical study of the sensitivity of the analysis to these assumptions, there seems to be little prospect of developing a formal theory to cover this aspect of the art of model building.

Third, the problem of assessing the adequacy of the model falls into the completely classical framework of goodness-of-fit tests. As soon as an alternative model is contemplated, the model is thereby generalized; after consideration of the evidence one may decide to use the simpler model (even if it is "significantly" inadequate in certain ways); but at some stage an assessment must be made without any alternative model (or at best a very ill-defined one) being postulated.

Fourth, it is unquestionable that the viewpoint adopted by the authors has resulted in a beautifully organized analysis, the components of which are clearly distinguishable and hence separately assessable. However, I do not ascribe this success solely to the Bayesian approach. In Chapter 5 Mosteller and Wallace (1964) contrast their analysis with a "classical linear discriminant study" in which weights $\{w_i\}$ are obtained such that the linear function

$$d = \Sigma w_i x_i$$

takes widely different values when applied to passages by Madison and by Hamilton, where x_i is the rate of use of word i in the passage of text studied. In this study Mosteller and Wallace chose to ignore the evidence relating to the distribution of word counts (Poisson or negative binomial); instead they assumed approximately normal distributions, which necessitated estimating means and variances separately. I see no reason why a frequentist should not be willing to use distributional information and a sufficiency argument and hence choose to rely on a discriminant function of the form (under the Poisson assumption)

$$d = \Sigma x_i \log(\hat{\mu}_{Hi}/\hat{\mu}_{Mi})$$

where $\hat{\mu}_{Hi}, \hat{\mu}_{Mi}$ are estimated rates for Hamilton and Madison respectively. Following this line of thought, it appears that a frequentist might well be led to use a discriminator closely similar to the one that Mosteller and Wallace use as a direct indicator of log odds. However, he would draw his inferences by comparing values of the discriminator with reference distributions such as are described in the first two lines of Table 5.1 below, which has been extracted from Tables 4.8.4. and 4.8.5.

TABLE 5.1

SUMMARY STATISTICS FOR
ADJUSTED TOTAL LOG ODDS, BASED ON COUNTS OF 30 WORDS,
NEGATIVE BINOMIAL MODEL

	Mean	*Standard Deviation*
48 Hamilton papers	17.1	5.3
50 Madison papers	−16.5	4.9
12 Disputed papers	−16.2	4.9
Disputed paper #55	− 6.1	

Note: All log odds are adjusted to a paper length of 2000 words.

From the table, we see that the "adjusted log odds" varies substantially among the various papers of known authorship; it seems proper that this variability should be taken into account in assessing the weight to be attached to the figures for the disputed papers.[9] However, the conflict between the Bayesian and classical approaches is not as great as may appear, since the Bayesian analysis can be interpreted, approximately, as being based directly on these same reference distributions. To see this, consider a simpler but analogous problem, in which we have two alternative hypotheses, under which an observable x has densities $f(x)$, $g(x)$ respectively. Then under the first (second) hypothesis, the likelihood ratio statistic $t(x) = \log(f(x)/g(x))$ will have some density $f^*(t)(g^*(t))$, say. These are the "reference distributions" for t. Now treating t as the observable, the log likelihood ratio becomes $t^*(t) = \log(f^*(t)/g^*(t))$, which is found to be identically equal to t. Thus the observed value of t gives simultaneously the likelihood ratio between the original f and g and the likelihood ratio between the reference distributions f^* and g^*. In the Federalist study, f and g have to be estimated, but the distributions summarized in the first two rows of Table 5.1 should exhibit the relationship described above, at least approximately. Assuming normality for these two distributions, we find that t^* is 20 to 25 percent larger than t in modulus throughout the interesting region. Except for this discrepancy, the complete Bayesian analysis is equivalent to one based solely on the two reference distributions summarized in Table 5.1.

6. USING THE STATISTICAL MODEL: IRRELEVANCE

I want to point out a way in which it seems to me that existing theories of inference are inadequate, even in a situation as favorable

[9] The next paragraph was added subsequent to the symposium.

as that of the Federalist study. Notice that the problem in this case is not that of coming to a decision regarding the authorship of the disputed papers, but rather that of summarizing the evidence one way or the other. Here, the statistician's role is that of the attorney (or rather that of both attorneys), not that of the judge.

How is the fitted model used? The argument can be expressed in the following way. Consider again the above interpretation of what the model says in terms of drawing a passage of text at random from the whole of the available population. Then the assumption is made that if one of the disputed papers had in fact been written by Madison, and if the rates of usage of the chosen set of words are computed for this paper, then there should be no way of distinguishing these rates from what they would be if a sample of known Madison text were to be drawn randomly. Similarly for Hamilton.

Expressed this way the assumption can be recognized as being an application of a principle known variously as the "principle of insufficient reason," or the "permutability postulate" of W. E. Johnson, which has been expounded with great force by De Finetti and Savage as a basis for statistical inference. I think it lies at the heart of all statistical work. However, the selection effect raises its head again, in a new guise. The permutability postulate is entertained for a *selected* aspect of the data, and not for the whole of the data. (If one were to take into account more of the available evidence concerning a disputed paper, for example its serial number, then it would certainly be distinguishable from the body of text of known Madison authorship, and one would not be able to use a statistical argument at all.) The assumption is that the rest of the evidence is irrelevant to the matter under discussion, and the explicit decision is made to ignore it for the sake of being able to use a statistical argument.[10]

My point here is that the computed probabilities, and the likelihoods that are the end product of a Bayesian analysis, depend on the particular selection that is made; so (in my view) these likelihoods should be regarded as conditional and not absolute. For similar reasons I am not in sympathy with the opinion that I must necessarily hold some degree of belief (or have proper betting odds) for any hypothesis that is presented to me.

---

[10] As it was put by Bartlett (1965), p. 402, "The statistical approach cannot by its nature deal with the unique sample—it must contemplate statistical variation which often from the Bayesian angle is irrelevant. The statistician can attempt to reduce the effect of irrelevant variation by conditional inferences and the like, but he cannot eliminate all questions of sampling variability or he has no probability distribution to work with at all."

It is not that the model (or reference set of comparable events) may be inaccurately known; but that the fact that the decision has been made to use this particular model is not allowed for in any way in a formal analysis.[11]

7. CHOOSING A PRIOR DISTRIBUTION

I would like to point out two areas of research in Bayesian methodology that seem to warrant further attention. First, the question of the choice of prior in cases where empirical data is sparse. I am disturbed by the existence of examples that seem to suggest a logical difficulty that a subjective Bayesian might meet in maintaining a vague state of mind about a large number of things simultaneously. I refer to the situations discussed by Stein (1959) (many normal means) and by Dempster (1963) (covariance matrix of a multinormal distribution with a barely adequate number of observations).

In the first case, one has observations $x_1, x_2, \ldots, x_n$ distributed independently and normally with unit variances about unknown means $\mu_1, \mu_2, \ldots, \mu_n$. If one sets up a uniform (quasi-) prior distribution for the point $(\mu_1, \ldots, \mu_n)$ in n-dimensional space, one gets perfectly satisfactory posterior distributions for each μ_i separately, and for any linear function $\Sigma a_i \mu_i$. However, the quantity $\theta = \Sigma \mu_i^2$ is assigned a posterior distribution that (if n is large) can be grossly at variance with the data. From ordinary sampling theory one expects $\Sigma x_i^2 \approx n + \theta$, but in the posterior distribution $\theta \approx n + \Sigma x_i^2$. Is it possible to set up a prior distribution that avoids this difficulty? If so, it would not be translation-invariant; what if one still believed the situation to be invariant?

Dempster's example is that of a random sample of size $n + 1$ points from a multinormal distribution in p dimensions, with p large but $n - p$ not large with respect to p. Let the unknown covariance matrix be (Σ_{ij}) with inverse (Σ^{ij}), and the sample estimate of it be $(n^{-1}S_{ij})$ with

[11] In developing a theory of inference in terms of "degrees of support," Hacking (1965) bases much of the argument on a "principle of irrelevance," but this seems not to be directly relevant here. This principle says (roughly) that *if* a certain piece of evidence is irrelevant to belief in a certain hypothesis, *then* the degree of support for the hypothesis is the same whether the evidence is included or suppressed. This does not help us decide whether any piece of evidence is irrelevant, unless we already have a probability specification and can compute likelihoods, when a previously stated principle (the "law of likelihood") can be invoked. *This* principle is similar to the sufficiency principle, and allows us to ignore any evidence that does not change the likelihoods.

inverse (nS^{ij}). According to direct sampling theory one has

$$S_{ii}/\Sigma_{ii} \sim \chi^2_n, \qquad \Sigma^{ii}/S^{ii} \sim \chi^2_{n-p+1},$$

so that S_{ii}/Σ_{ii} is stochastically larger than Σ^{ii}/S^{ii}. However, Dempster shows that for any linearly invariant prior distribution, in the posterior distribution one has Σ^{ii}/S^{ii} stochastically larger than S_{ii}/Σ_{ii}. The discrepancy can be substantial. Thus again the Bayesian with a "diffuse" prior may obtain a posterior distribution that in many ways is in flat contradiction of some clear indications of the data.

One can argue that in some sense (though I know of no completely satisfactory definition) S_{ii} is sufficient for Σ_{ii}, and S^{ii} for Σ^{ii}; it would seem reasonable to base inferences for Σ_{ii} and Σ^{ii} on the marginal likelihoods of their respective sufficient statistics. But this sacrifices consistency.

Another source of discomfort with methods that depend at all strongly on prior assumptions is the possibility of disastrous mistakes if the assumptions are ill-founded. Stone (1963) has studied some aspects of this problem, and elsewhere Mallows (1968). I have examined several techniques for choosing the coefficients in a multiple linear regression analysis. A brief summary of some of the results follows.

Suppose that observations $(y_j, \mathbf{x}_j)$ where $\mathbf{x}_j = (x_{1j}, \ldots, x_{kj})$ are available and it is believed that the usual linear regression model

$$y_j = \sum_i \beta_i x_{ij} + e_j = \boldsymbol{\beta}^T x_j + e_j$$

is appropriate, the errors (e_j) being independent, with zero means and common known variance, which we take as unity. We regard the x's as fixed. Corresponding to any proposed technique for choosing fitted coefficients $\mathbf{b} = (b_1, \ldots, b_k)$, let us compute the quantity

$$R = E\left(\sum_j (\mathbf{b}^T\mathbf{x}_j - \boldsymbol{\beta}^T\mathbf{x}_j)^2\right).$$

This is the mean square error of the fitted regression function, summed over the observed points, and it is an attractive measure of the adequacy of the proposed technique. Supposing that the design is orthogonal and standardized so that

$$\sum_j \mathbf{x}_j\mathbf{x}_j{}^T = I_k),$$

we find that for several simple rules we have

$$R = \sum_i m(\beta_i)$$

FIGURE 5.1

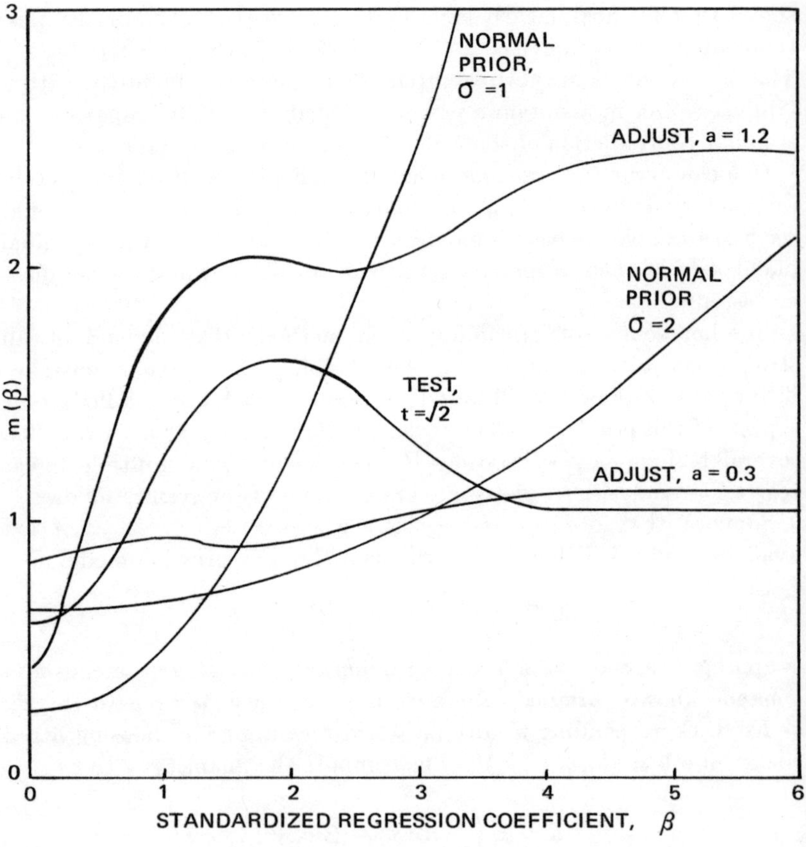

where the function $m(\beta)$ is symmetric about $\beta = 0$. Several examples are exhibited in Figure 5.1, where the rules considered are as follows:

1. Bayesian estimates corresponding to independent normal priors with mean zero and variance $\sigma^2 = 1$.
2. Similarly with $\sigma^2 = 4$.
3. (Not shown.) Least-squares on all coefficients. Here $m = 1$ identically.

4. Retain only those least-squares coefficients that are significantly different from zero at the level $\alpha = 15.73$ percent, i.e., whose t-statistics exceed $\sqrt{2}$ in magnitude.[12]

5. & 6. Use least-squares estimates adjusted towards zero by a fixed amount a (if less than a in magnitude, replace by zero).[13]

From inspection of the figure, we see that the assumption of a normal prior leaves no margin for error. The "adjust" strategy buys very little. The "test" strategy works well if the majority of the β's are either very large (so that these terms are infallibly included) or else very small (so that zero is a better estimate than the least-squares estimate). If the majority of the β's are in the range $1 \leq |\beta| \leq 3$ this rule can be much worse than simple least-squares.

The existence of these results, and a reluctance on my part to trust results that depend on poorly supported assumptions, lead me to suggest that it might be useful to study the sampling properties of Bayesian methods, as well as their sensitivity to changes in the prior assumptions and the data distributions.

8. ROBUST BAYESIANISM

Another area that seems worthy of study concerns the use of Bayesian methods based not as usual on the likelihood of the data given the hypotheses, since these likelihoods might be subject to specification error to an indeterminate degree, but on likelihoods of statistics that are more robust (in the frequentist's sense) than the (theoretically sufficient) statistic. For a trivial example, take the location-parameter problem, with a locally uniform prior. If a normal specification is assumed and an ordered sample $x_1, x_2, \ldots, x_n$ is available, the usual posterior is a t distribution with $n - 1$ degrees of freedom. Suppose, however, that we do not trust the normal specification, but are willing to rely on a symmetry assumption. Then for any hypothetical mean μ we can appeal to the distribution-free statistic "number of x's that are less than μ," which would be distributed binomially with $p = \frac{1}{2}$. Hence we derive a likelihood function that is discontinuous at

---

[12] This value is presented because of its relevance to a graphical technique presented in Mallows (1968) for comparing subset regression equations. Other choices give functions of the same general shape, becoming more and more exaggerated as α decreases.

[13] This is almost equivalent to assuming a double-exponential prior with density $\frac{1}{2}a \exp -a|\beta|$.

each observation and constant between the observations, taking the value $2^{-n}\,{}^{n}C_j$ between x_j and x_{j+1}.

Much of the recent work on robust location estimation can be carried over directly to the Bayesian framework, but it is not clear how to proceed for nonlocation parameters.

DISCUSSION

· *Meyer*: Professor Cornfield, would you like to start off with some general comments?

· *Cornfield*: Let me talk a little bit about what attracted me to Bayesian methods.

For 20 years or so, I have been more or less a practicing or consulting statistician. My output was supposed to be advice on the design and analysis of experiments and investigations, and it never was contemplated that I would have any strong theoretical ideas other than those necessary to do my main job. It has been interesting for me to look back to see how this Bayesian orientation to which I now have a deep commitment has developed over the years.

The first set of problems that set me to wondering if I really knew what I was doing, in a classical context, was a set of problems all involving estimation in some sense. Fisher had given us methods of maximum likelihood estimation which were very attractive and were very well defined. One could always knock out an answer, and in most cases, it was an answer that seemed reasonable, except every now and then one ran across a problem where there seemed to be something wrong with the answer. If people want to press me I can give a few examples, but this set me to wondering about the bases of estimation. When one started to dig into the literature one found theoretical disagreement on the part of maximum likelihood estimators. There was one example that confused me greatly which showed that even asymptotically the maximum likelihood estimators were not consistent in cases of regular estimation. This was one puzzle.

Another set of puzzles that I accumulated in the course of this kind of work was a set arising from the existence of nuisance parameters. In general, if one is doing hypothesis testing or interval estimation on some complicated function of parameters, one would like a test or an interval that has certain frequency properties no matter what the values of the other parameters that do not particularly pertain. One example of this is in the investigation of vaccines. A parameter that is always of great interest is the effectiveness of the vaccine. If one looks at how this is defined, essentially what it turns out to be is one minus the ratio of the incidence of the disease among those not vaccinated to the incidence of the disease among those vaccinated. This last is the ratio of two binomial parameters, and we may like confidence limits on this ratio. I don't know if anyone has ever proved that no confidence limits exist that are independent of the individual values of P_1 and P_2, but for all the things you tried, you couldn't say the interval you obtained included the true ratio with the stated frequency no matter what the values of the individual P's. It seemed very strange that the basic formulation, which I considered the frequency formulation in those days, seemed to be incapable in principle of getting an exact answer to what seemed like a fairly simple question, "How effective is the vaccine?"

One very well known instance of this problem of nuisance parameters is given by the Behrens-Fisher problem where you want to compare the same interval estimate of the difference between two normal means when the standard deviations of the two populations are not assumed to be equal. The problem is that the frequency with which the interval covers the true difference depends on the unknown ratio of standard deviations.

In my case, a very important influence in my thinking was to read the series of papers that appeared in the *Journal of the Royal Statistical Society* initiated by R. A. Fisher's criticism of the set of intervals that appeared in the *Biometrika* tables that in turn went back to a test developed by Welch and Aspin. This was an attempt to solve this particular problem of nuisance parameters and, in one sense if one doesn't get too rigorous about it, it was a completely successful solution. Welch and Aspin were able to demonstrate by numerical methods that the interval they tabulated did, in fact, cover the difference of means with stated frequency no matter what the values of the nuisance parameters. This interval was different from the interval that Fisher had worked out using fiducial methods. Fisher published a criticism of this which made a point which I had never seen made before, though

I have since realized that it has been in the literature for a long time. What Fisher said in effect was that it may be true in fact that the interval sample space is broken down into subsets, and if we look at the ratio of the standard deviations of some given quantity, the question is "How frequently will this interval cover the true value in that subset of samples?" The answer to that question depends on the true ratio of the standard deviations and Fisher was able to exhibit subsets in which the P percent confidence interval covered the true value, say less than P percent of the time, no matter what the true ratio of standard deviations. Welch and Aspin said, "That doesn't bother us because we weren't setting out to cover it in subsets." I think Fisher's argument was that if that is the subset you happen to be in, what is the point of having an interval that you know will be right less than P percent of the time for that subset? I think this came very close to the heart of putting the finger on the basic difficulty in applying the frequency outlook to scientific experimentation. No matter what this kind of interval with an appropriate confidence coefficient was supposed to do, it seemed hard to say that you have 95 percent confidence in the interval when, in fact, you knew for the subset you were in that the interval was going to cover the true value interval 90 percent, say, or less of the time no matter what the values of the nuisance parameters. A number of years later, I was talking to Jimmy Savage about this, and he gave a more extreme example. This is another standard problem involving a confidence interval on the ratio of two means. There is a well-known solution which is usually attributed to Feiller which has the property of covering the true ratio, no matter what it is, with the standard frequency. Unfortunately, for any given sample you can find a confidence coefficient such that the interval is minus infinity to plus infinity, and Savage said, "What does it mean to say you are only 95 percent confident that the true ratio is between plus and minus infinity?"

A third set of problems is the set that I talked about in my paper, which is the effect of the sequential path by which you reach your observations and the effect of this sequential path on the conclusion you draw from the observations. I have given an example in the paper of a hypothetical investigator who has done an experiment and has tried to test his results, but finds he doesn't quite have the significance level that his editor insists on before he will publish the paper. He comes to the statistician and asks how many more observations he should make. Of course, if you think about that for a while you see that from a frequency point of view, at least from one frequency point of view, this two-stage experiment is incapable of ever achieving the desired significance level. Suppose the man wanted to test at the 5 percent significance level and had decided in his own mind that if after the first stage he had achieved significance, he would say there was a difference. If he didn't achieve significance, he would come to the statistician and ask him how many more observations he should make. If the hypothesis being tested is in fact true, he is certain to reject it with a frequency greater than 5 percent. I didn't quite make up this example since somebody came to me with exactly this problem. I was conscious of this dilemma, and I told him how many more observations I would take if I were in his boots, but it was an unsettling experience. You think you have a firm theoretical guide, and you find that time after time you have to put it aside and take a closer look since it is giving the wrong answer in this case. I think the particular example of this type that really convinced me that something is fundamentally wrong was when I was trying to help out a friend of mine by saving him observations by suggesting that he do some sequential testing. I said, "Let's do the sequential t test." He had been testing hypotheses with fixed sample sizes, using perhaps a dozen animals, and said, "Gee, we ought to be able to save a lot on that," so I wrote down an alpha and beta, specified the nature of the standardized difference for the alternative, and then went to the National Bureau of Standard Tables to see what the limits would be. It turned out that he couldn't stop with a dozen observations no matter what the observations showed, and if you look at the National Bureau of Standard Tables this is, in fact, a characteristic. For any given alpha, beta, and standardized difference, you have to take a certain minimum number of observations before you can begin to decide to stop, accept the hypothesis or reject it no matter what the observations show. This really did seem like a caricature of drawing conclusions from data, and I now believe that the reason for this is that the parameter space that is specified by the sequential t test is much too primitive. It specifies a particular value, if the known hypothesis is true and specifies a particular alternative and, in fact, if that corresponded to the situation I was faced with, it would be reasonable to behave as the National Bureau of Standard Tables tells you to behave. In fact, the reason it is regarded as preposterous is that you are quite willing to admit a whole family of alternatives, and the procedure is inappropriate if you do have a whole family of alternatives.

· *Geisser:* Well, for ten years I was subjected to the sort of table talk that you just heard. I was a colleague of Jerry's during that period and I was going through, with him, the catharsis of changing from a regular statistician to a Bayesian statistician for many of these reasons. Of course, I am a little younger than Jerry and I am waiting for a better post-Bayesian period to see what will occur there.

I think the most critical thing for me was Fisher's book *Statistical Methods and Scientific Inference.** All his criticisms of the standard procedures and his ideas and thoughts on what he was trying to do more or less convinced me that you are really interested in a posterior distribution of a parameter. I think Fisher always was interested in that. He just, perhaps very wisely, refused to pay the price of a prior distribution. Also, particularly in the problems of classification-discrimination, it seems to me the Bayesian approach is much more natural. It actually answers the question that the investigator asks in these problems, which is, how likely is this observation to come from this or that population rather than the standard solution which sort of just decides to put the observation in a pigeonhole based on some error rates without saying anything in particular about the observation in hand?

· *Hill:* I am just going to describe the basic points of my paper. One of the points I was trying to illustrate was that there are very real differences between Bayesian inference and more classical inference, both confidence and fiducial. In the variance components example, this occurs when the usual estimator of the between variance component is quite negative. The Bayesian winds up with a virtually flat likelihood function for that parameter, whereas both Fisher and those people who wrote on the problem from the confidence interval point of view felt that when you get a very negative value for the usual estimator, then that is strong evidence that the true component is small, or may be even exactly zero.

The second point that I was trying to illustrate relates to the question that is raised by Dr. Mallows of the introduction of a new parameter, perhaps one that you hadn't thought of before seeing the data, which to my mind is natural for a Bayesian and which fits in entirely within the scheme of Bayesian inference. The particular case I am talking about is where you may wish to introduce a negative correlation between the residuals in the same row in this one-way analysis of variance and, if you do this, you wind up with a very different inference about everything. For one thing, there may now be strong evidence that the between variance component is small. There may or may not be, and it depends not only on the value of the estimate but on both the sum of squares within and between individually.

* Fisher (1956).

Let me say a word or two on this general question of the introduction of a new parameter. In principle, it seems to me that a Bayesian is in effect describing what he would do given any set of data—what inference he would make given any conceivable set of observations. Now, obviously, in practice he can't quite do this in a literal sense because it would be infinitely time consuming. Nonetheless, it seems to me the right goal at which to aim. From this point of view there is no real difference whether you say you observed this unusual set of data and have therefore brought in a new parameter to account for it, or whether before observing the data you consider all possible samples, and conditional on each such sample, decide what your inference would be. Of course there is always some practical advantage in having had enough foresight to consider beforehand an appropriate course of action in the event of a negative value of the estimator, since you are then less likely to be overly swayed by such data when it occurs. But I don't see any fundamental difference. In any event it isn't the data that is suggesting to me the idea of introducing a new parameter; I could equally well have done this by simply considering what inference I would draw conditional on such data before actually observing it.

· *Lindley:* The paper I prepared for this meeting is divided into two parts; the first part is a general discussion of Bayesian ideas, and the second is the application of them to a particular problem. First of all, let me say something about Bayesian ideas in general, particularly to emphasize one point which I want to emphasize because I don't know of any decent reply to this point.

We have been engaged already this morning in personal history, and I would like to do the same. When I was an undergraduate, I was taught my statistics by Harold Jeffreys, who was, and still is, a Bayesian, and he had to plead with us to believe in prior distributions. Since those days there has been a great change because arguments have been produced to show that if you are going to be sensible at all, you've just got to be a Bayesian. Ramsey's original argument was that if a person is going to act in at all a sensible way, he has just got to act as if he had a probability distribution over the unknown states of the world. This argument has been refined and modified by several people—De Finetti, Savage, and others, and put into what seems to me a very elegant form by Pratt, Raifa, and Schlaifer in the *Journal of the American Statistical Association.** Now this argument seems to me to be absolutely compelling. Some axioms are stated for rational behavior, and deductions are made from these. I have never seen any argument that suggests that

* Pratt *et al.* (1964).

the deductions are wrong, and there have been very few arguments that suggest the axioms are not reasonable ones. Therefore, from this point of view it seems everybody has got to be a Bayesian. Bayesian ideas also enable us to tackle problems such as the design of experiments which haven't been tackled in a very coherent way beforehand. They just couldn't have been tackled because if you are going to design an experiment, the only information you have is your prior information, and if you are going to deny the prior information to be quantified, you are going to be in a bit of difficulty designing an experiment, at any rate using quantitative ideas.

I do mention two aspects of the Bayesian argument that personally cause me some trouble. The first thing is the sort of problem that comes under goodness of fit. I myself don't know how this fits into a Bayesian framework. There is rather a brief dismissal of the difficulties by Hill in his paper. I don't understand his argument because there was a time in the history of science when everyone knew in a commonsense way that Newtonian dynamics just didn't work. It was wrong. Anybody in his right frame of mind would say it is impossible, but there was no alternative hypothesis to put into its place, until Einstein came along with an alternative. There was a period of history when the null hypothesis of Newtonian dynamics would have been rejected under any sensible system, and there was no alternative. That sort of system is hard for a Bayesian to understand. He has to admit that it is true, just from empirical observation, and yet it is very hard to formulate it, because you need to put a prior distribution over the alternatives and there just aren't any alternatives that anybody has been bright enough to think about.

The second difficulty in the Bayesian approach that I mention is the nonparametric one, and I do make some suggestions. In discussion with Jimmy Savage this past week, I understand that the suggestion I made doesn't work. Bruce Hill* has been there before me and discovered that it doesn't work, so the suggestion that I have in the paper won't be satisfactory.

I would like to make one point about the particular problem in my paper. It is concerned with the multiple regression of one variable on a large number of others, and the sort of educational application I had in mind is where the dependent variable is a person's ability in some sense, and the measurements, the independent variables, are tests that you make. The problem I considered is where you want to predict a person's ability and the question you ask yourself is, "Which tests are really

* [See Hill (1968)].

worth giving him?" Now, such a situation fits into the linear multiple regression framework and like that, it asks a particular question, "How am I to make this prediction, and what are the variables that I should measure to make this prediction?" If it fits into that form you can put it into a decision framework and you can get a Bayesian solution. You can turn the handle and out comes an answer.

This is the sort of procedure that appeals to me, and it ought to appeal to most of us in this computer age. There is a program here, a systematic way of attacking a problem of this sort. You don't have to scratch your head and think of some nice intuitive statistic that looks good and do things like that. If you are clever, that's fine, but if you are like me and you are not very clever, it is far better to have a machine to turn the handle and produce an answer. In this case, it is quite interesting that the answer agrees with a suggestion of Dr. Mallows'. He gave full treatment of this problem. But it also shows me that I can't get Dr. Mallows' answer unless I make a lot of assumptions. Many of these assumptions seem to me to be highly relevant. One shouldn't apply this *CP* plot of Dr. Mallows', for example, unless one is sure that these assumptions are reasonably satisfied. This is quite an advantage of the Bayesian method. It gives a procedure that one can carry through to produce an answer under a well-defined set of circumstances.

· *Mallows:* I would like to start by reading my first sentence: "I believe that my participation in this symposium was invited in an attempt to provide some counterweight (not to say opposition) to the other speakers." I feel myself to be an outlier in this group if only for the reason that I don't think of myself as committed to a Bayesian position or to any other position. It seems to me the world is rather more complicated than it is sometimes made to look when you view it through Bayesian spectacles or decision theory spectacles. Maybe my experience is not typical, but I have come across many problems with which I feel very unsure as to just what the right specification is, what the right parameters are, and certainly what the prior distribution ought to be. So I don't see at the moment that all my problems are going to be solved by the Bayesian creed. I've tried to give some examples in my paper of cases where it seems to me the frequentist attitude is useful. The main problem is the one of deciding when your model is adequate, where you have a null hypothesis and no clearly defined alternative. This seems to me to be quite common when you are faced with a new situation. When you are in a well-defined situation in which you have a lot of experience, then certainly you can model it and you ought to model it in as complete a way as you can. If you have frequency information about various parameters, then you surely ought to be able to model that by a prior distribution, which is what I believe Mosteller and Wallace did in their study of *The Federalist** authorship problem. They fitted a model, postulated some parameters and then collected some pertinent data to see how the parameters varied, and they described this by what they call a prior distribution fitted to the data.

Where the Bayesian does differ from a frequentist is that he is willing to make assumptions which are not directly based on data; that is to say, they are based on opinions without any clear basis from where these opinions come. It is very difficult to argue against this position, because certainly once you accept that this is a valid thing to do then all the world fits into this framework. My criticism of it is the same that can be leveled against decision theory. All problems, if you are willing to formalize them sufficiently, can be viewed as decision theory problems. You have a prior assumption of the way the world is, and you have various costs according to what you do, and you just turn the handle and out comes the right action. The difficulty with applying this is that you usually don't have enough solid information to apply the method. So, it seems to me a very tentative attitude is a proper one. I learned my statistics at University College from Egon Pearson. My credo has been stated by him in many places, namely, that what we all ought to be doing is to try to find out how we can best help one another and not to say, "This is the way to do all problems and if you don't agree with me, you are wrong."

I mention toward the end of the paper a couple of areas in which it seems to me further research would be useful. I am unhappy with the argument that says once you've got a posterior distribution, that is the end of the problem. It still seems I don't know quite what to do. If you give me a posterior distribution of a parameter, I still am not quite clear what this means, how I convey this information, and what action I ought to make; so the sampling theory behavior of procedures derived by Bayesian methods are of interest. Another thing that worries me is the sensitivity of Bayesian methods to the prior assumptions. Sometimes too little attention is paid to how disastrously stupid a procedure can be if you make the wrong assumptions. Finally, I make a suggestion which relates to robust Bayesianism. I won't go into detail on it at this point.

---

* Mosteller and Wallace (1963).

· *Cornfield*: I would like to talk a little bit about Professor Lindley's remarks on goodness-of-fit. I have seen this recurring statement that Bayesian procedures seem to be having trouble handling the idea of goodness-of-fit, with no clearly specified alternatives, and I am not sure that I see the difficulty. Let's take the phrase, goodness-of-fit, and let's suppose there is some scientific hypothesis like the Newtonian one which essentially specifies the values of parameters for a series of discrete situations. What one does is make, let's say, independent observations for each one of these situations, observations which have a frequency distribution that depends on the values of the parameters being specified by the hypothesis. Now, one has to make up a table of two columns. One column is going to have in it the values of the parameters specified by the hypothesis. The second column is going to have in it the observations. The question is, "Can Bayesian methods say whether this is good or bad?" It seems to me the way to formalize this is to write a third column. If the first column is false—the first hypothesis is false—then the alternative that we want to consider is the set of values specified in the third column. We would have no trouble with the Bayesian procedures. The difficulty is we can't specify that third column. It seems that a very reasonable way to proceed is to take this hypothesis specified by the values in the first column and proceeding informally for the moment assign to it a nonzero prior probability. You may have trouble deciding that value but let's put that difficulty aside for the moment. Now, since we don't have any clear idea of the alternatives, let's consider we have probability, p, assigned to the hypothesis under test, and we have one minus p left over. The question is, what are we going to do with that one minus p? A reasonable thing to do is to say that if the hypothesis is false, and if we have no clear idea of the alternatives, we will assign a very diffuse prior distribution to the value of the parameter. Or put more concretely, if the hypothesis says the value of the parameter is seven, and you assign .1 probability to seven then we have .9 left over, and for that .9, we will say the parameter has a very diffuse distribution, perhaps normal, from plus to minus infinity, with a very big standard deviation. With those assumptions we can now calculate the posterior probability of the hypothesis in the light of the observations and the specified diffuse set of alternatives.

· *Lindley*: What is this parameter in a Newtonian situation?

· *Cornfield*: Oh, say it's the distance between,the number of miles between,two degrees of parallel, to take one famous case. The Newtonian hypothesis specified, "Given some other observations, if you measured the number of miles between the 40th and 41st parallel, you would get a certain number," and for a long time Newton didn't publish the *Principia* because there was a bad observation that somebody had made and the number of miles was inconsistent with the prediction of the theory.

· *Geisser*: Is that really a goodness-of-fit problem? You parametrized it.

· *Cornfield*: I parametrized it in what I regard as a reasonable way when you have no clear idea of what the alternatives are. In that case it could be almost anything if it is not what I say it is.

· *Lindley*: But in that situation all values of the parameters would have been impossible. Newtonian theory predicted that the distance should have been 41 miles, you know, and you got 42 miles. The other values of the parameter were even more unlikely.

· *Cornfield*: I don't follow that. Suppose the Newtonian theory predicted 41 and you would have said, well, there was a class of alternatives, one member of that class is that it is 42, and we have such a precise measurement on the distance that the probability that it is really 41 is very low, so we have to reject that hypothesis.

· *Lindley*: Suppose the maximum was at 45 and now I go away to some other part of the world where the number should have been 67, but I measure and I find it is 72. The 74 and the 45 couldn't be produced by any single theory. In other words, you are saying the 41 won't work, it should be 45, and the 67 won't work because it should have been 72, but I can't offer you any explanation as to why you get the 72 and the 45. There is nothing to put in its place.

· *Cornfield*: Well, I see what you are saying, but let me persist in my naïvete. What would happen in such a situation? One would say it ought to be 41, we have made a measurement and the measurement is inconsistent with any set of prior probabilities so it is not 41; we have to put this aside, and now since we have a measurement of 43, we have now progressed to the hypothesis that perhaps it is 43 in some other part of the world and, by gosh, it's 75, and we have to reject that hypothesis too. Well, the goodness-of-fit test has permitted us to reject a well-formulated hypothesis. It's permitted us to tentatively formulate another one and we have now rejected that. The next step I think would be to say, well maybe the distance depends on the degree of latitude. Now, we are getting a more complicated hypothesis which we could, in turn, test and presumably reject, until somebody came along who thought of the right one. I see there is a difficulty in finding what scientific truth is in a complicated situation, but I don't see what the form of mathematical difficulty is in getting the goodness-of-fit test.

· *Hill*: I don't see what it is either, and I think 30 years ago Jeffreys* fundamentally suggested this approach to testing hypotheses, and it would have been a good thing if it hadn't been ignored for 30 years. One point I think is important is that typically a decent scientific hypothesis doesn't specify the value of a parameter. I believe it typically says something about what you think about the parameter in a distributional sense. To take a less sophisticated example than that of Newtonian mechanics, consider an industrial process. A kind of quality control problem, which usually produces normal measurements with mean zero and known standard deviation of one. It goes along and you are concerned when there is evidence of a serious change in the level of production. Classically, statisticians would tend to set this up as a null hypothesis that this location parameter is zero against an alternative that might be one of a great variety, that is, it might say that almost anything could happen if the null hypothesis weren't true or it might be more specific. It would be wrong to think of the null hypothesis as the statement that the parameter has value zero because the hypothesis actually is the statement that production is continuing as usual. The null hypothesis is that we are under the usual conditions of production. The important difference is that the null hypothesis has positive prior probability whereas a hypothesis to the effect that a parameter is zero will typically have zero probability and isn't worth considering.

What about the alternatives? The job of the statistician is to think of alternatives. In this problem, either the process is continuing as usual or something has happened. What's the alternative? If you know something about the process you might say the best alternative is that Jones, who runs the machine, is drunk or any other alternative that you can formulate for yourself. When you begin to think in this way, you can proceed to calculate posterior odds for the null hypothesis against one or more of these various alternatives. There may be many alternatives, not just that Jones is drunk, but that the machine slipped a gear. I don't see the conceptual difficulty in this kind of hypothesis testing goodness-of-fit.

· *Lindley*: Because I think you can run out of alternatives and yet still feel there is something wrong! You should say, "I don't know how this world's moving around, what the mechanics are, but I know it's not Newtonian."

---

* See Jeffreys (1961).

· *Cornfield*: Why is that a difficulty for Bayesian goodness-of-fit? All I would ask from a statistical analysis is that you quantify the fact that something is wrong. You don't have an explanation that is consistent with the facts. If a Bayesian procedure can do that . . . .

· *Lindley*: It can't.

· *Geisser*: It seems to me there is nothing wrong in a situation like this with a simple significance test.

· *Hill*: What good does it do?

· *Cornfield*: That is what I want to avoid because I don't like simple significance tests. That alternative I must say fills me with a sort of philosophical horror, this kind of dualism. For certain kinds of problems, sample space doesn't matter, but for other kinds of problems . . . .

· *Mallows*: All problems are not the same.

· *Cornfield*: Consider what a goodness-of-fit test is. You have to invent a statistic.

· *Mallows*: Specifying a statistic is just about the same thing as specifying a class of alternatives because you can generate for yourself an artificial class of alternatives by parametrizing the thing according to the statistic you have chosen to use. What I was trying to point out in my paper here was not that you have a model and you choose a statistic to test goodness-of-fit; you have data and you look at the data and you see clearly without any formal procedure that it just doesn't work. What do you do? You may invent your statistic after seeing the data. That doesn't fit into any classical goodness-of-fit procedures either. That is what I find wrong with formal procedures. If I'm against anything, I'm against formality, which for me includes both Bayesianism and classical methods.

· *Hill*: This is a different point. I feel that the examples you introduce on the "many location parameters" mean something very different from what you think. First of all, we ought to start out by saying there are at least three different attitudes a person could have on which he would behave precisely the same way. One attitude is that the parameter really has such and such a prior distribution in a frequency sense. Another would be there is no such thing but only my personal opinions about the parameter. Still a third is that, I don't care anything about that, but I'm going to act as though the parameter had such and such a prior distribution. As soon as you recognize this, the examples you bring up are transparently fallacious, because to take this one about the sum of squares of the location parameters, your argument would seem to lead to the conclusion that no matter what data you get (since you don't say which kind of data is more unreasonable than any other) that the data in itself clearly contradicts this kind of inference. How can that be true unless you are ready to disprove Bayes' theorem as a mathematical fact of life? In fact, you yourself would have that same posterior distribution if the parameter had the prior distribution in question.

· *Mallows*: The question is whether this is a proper prior.

[*Editor's Note*: There ensued a discussion of the importance of improperness of the Jeffreys' uniform prior. Both Hill and Mallows agreed later that this was not the crucial point. Professor Hill and Dr. Mallows gave written replies, which follow.]

· *Hill*: Suppose that the prior distribution for the true vector of means $\underline{\mu}$ is uniform over the sphere, S, of radius, R, centered at the origin in n-dimensional Euclidian space, and that given $\underline{\mu}$, the observation vector, $\underline{X}$, is normally distributed with mean, $\underline{\mu}$, and covariance matrix known to be an identity matrix. For sufficiently large R, I will regard it as not improbable that I will observe a vector $\underline{X}$ such that the posterior distribution of $\underline{\mu}$, given $\underline{X}$, is very nearly that which would be obtained using the improper prior distribution of Jeffreys'.

The approximation will be good if $\underline{X}$ falls inside and not too near the boundary of S. For example, let $r^2(\alpha, n)$ be the upper $(1-\alpha)$ percentile of the chi-square distribution with n degrees of freedom. If $\|\underline{X}\| \le R - r(\alpha, n)$, then the sphere of radius $r(\alpha, m)$ centred at $\underline{X}$ will be contained in S, and the posterior density of $\underline{\mu}$ given such an $\underline{X}$ will be proportional to $\exp[-\frac{1}{2}\|\underline{X} - \underline{\mu}\|^2]$ for $\|\underline{\mu} - \underline{X}\| \le r(\alpha, n)$. If α is sufficiently small (so that $r(\alpha, n)$ is sufficiently large), then for all practical purposes this is the same as the normal posterior distribution of $\underline{\mu}$ based upon the improper Jeffreys' prior.

Finally, using this fixed value of $r(\alpha, n)$, (and the crucial point is that it is fixed and does not depend on R except that $r(\alpha, n) < R$), choose R sufficiently large so that $Pr[\|\underline{X}\| \le R - r(\alpha, n)]$ is large. Observe that this probability is the ratio of the volumes of two spheres with radii $R - r(\alpha, n)$ and R, respectively. This ratio approaches unity as R increases. Although the marginal distribution of $\underline{X}$ is not uniform over S, the above probability can also be made large (or at least non-negligible) in this same way, where we must now integrate over $\underline{\mu}$ to get the marginal distribution of $\underline{X}$.

Therefore, I do not believe it is either improperness or a "boundary phenomenon" which causes the difficulty with the prior distribution of Jeffreys'. Rather, it is the fact that in practice one is rarely sufficiently uniform over a sufficiently broad region in n-dimensional space to want to use this prior distribution.

In any case the data cannot speak out against the prior distribution in the way suggested by Dr. Mallows. See also Hill (1969) and its sequel.

· *Mallows*: I agree this is not the crucial point. I should have said that the question is whether such a prior-posterior pair, or the one described in section six of Stein (1962) corresponds adequately to a state of weak prior knowledge about several different things simultaneously, which is what I was discussing in my paper. In some ways they do, and in other ways they do not. I am still not convinced there is not a fundamental difficulty here, but propriety of the prior is not involved.

· *Lindley*: Let's take the problem of "between-within" analysis of variance. Suppose we have several means. Somebody tells me the value of the first mean is 42.6 and the value of the second is 51.3. I'm going to be pretty sure that the next mean he is going to tell me is somewhere around that sort of region. In other words, it is not going to be 10 to the 566. It's going to be in this 40–50 neighborhood because I know from experience that things that are heterogeneous to that sort of extent just don't get mixed up together. There is a sort of feeling all those means are roughly of the same order. In other words, they are correlated, and so it seems perfectly legitimate to put in a prior distribution that uses this past experience that I've got of living in the world, and that's why I want to put on a prior distribution which really has quite a lot of information. If those means concern educational testing it's not information about education I'm putting in, it's just information about the world in general. I'm still worried about the covariance example that you quote because nobody as far as I know has come up with a sensible prior, but again I have the feeling that if I knew one of the variances in this dispersion matrix, then I might have feelings about the other variances as well.

· *Mallows*: In that case, it is even more difficult because of the question of units.

· *Geisser*: You don't really want to say that they're in the same neighborhood when one may be in inches and the other may be in light-years.

· *Lindley*: Well, no, because I know very well that in experiments, people don't do that sort of thing. I've yet to meet an experimenter that comes along and says, "I've measured this first thing in microns, and measured the second in light-years."

· *Geisser*: Suppose they were height and weight?

· *Lindley*: If they were, I'd be absolutely astonished if somebody came along and said to me that Mr. Cornfield's height is 10 to the 27th.

· *Hill*: But you were talking about variances.

· *Lindley*: Well, say that his variance is 10 to the 27th. You don't measure things in that sort of unit, but if we were talking about astronomy, then all right.

· *Cornfield*: I certainly agree with Lindley that in most situations, things are in the same units; information on one gives you information about the other. But, we wouldn't argue that there aren't people in the world who would come to you with a set of numbers, one of which was a molecular weight of RNA and one of which was the unemployment rate in Syracuse, and if they came to you with such numbers, then they wouldn't mutually support each other. You would have independent priors for them. I fail to see the nature of the difficulty.

· *Lindley*: If somebody came along with data of a mixed-up sort like that, I, as a Bayesian, would make some pretty funny conclusions at first, until the data got so big I suddenly would realize what was happening.

· *Cornfield*: I, as a Bayesian, would ask why you are studying such diverse things, and once I understood that these were quite different things, I'd say that we have to have independent priors for these two and we would have to have a formulation that would be such that whatever you found out on the molecular weight of RNA had no influence on what you found out on the unemployment rate in Syracuse. This is simply a way of formalizing what seems to be a very common-sense way of looking at observations.

A number of people looking at Stein's original result had raised examples like this. Stein presented it from a non-Bayesian point of view, and his conclusion applied whether the measurements were on the same or different quantities. If one doesn't introduce priors, this does introduce a difficulty. It is hard to understand the scientific value of Stein's result, but the minute one says let's look at this from the point of view of priors, it all becomes very clear.

· *Hill*: Am I confused here? I thought in your paper you were arguing that data could show that a certain prior was foolish irrespective of what observations came out.

· *Mallows*: I am not ruling out any observations.

· *Hill*: You didn't say that. You didn't say that there were certain kinds of observations for which this would be true and others for which it wouldn't be true, which would be very reasonable.

· *Mallows*: That is so.

· *Hill*: But if you say that, it is well within the Bayesian framework of hypothesis testing, like Jeffreys' formulation, because if there were two different priors for the parameter, then the data will support one versus the other. Maybe it will leave them indifferent, but there is no difficulty from the Bayesian theory.

· *Mallows*: But the question here is that the data can seem to support the prior in one way and yet contradict it in another. This is the same prior.

· *Hill*: But that can't be true, because if that were true, that would contradict Bayes' theorem itself if the prior were the true prior.

· *Geisser*: Can we discuss another question that I had assumed bothered the Bayesian, randomization?

· *Cornfield*: It doesn't bother me. I don't know if I can say precisely why it doesn't bother me, but let me try.

The apparent difficulty is that randomization is very often a useful and important device. On the other hand, if one looks at this situation from the Bayesian point of view, what it seems to say is your inference depends on priors, and on your observations. Since you have priors on the values of, say, every individual in a finite population, it doesn't look as if randomization is going to affect your inference at all, so one may just as well use the same inference whether the data is at random or not random. Let's talk about this from the point of view of sampling from a finite population. Why should we take a random sample rather than any other kind of sample? As a Bayesian, I would say we started with a finite population and in principle, with a prior for every member. You have to say "in principle" because if you are sampling a population of 200 million people, you've got to have some simplifying assumptions to get on with the job. But, in principle, I have a prior for every person in the country, say for every one to two million people. Now you come along with a sample, and I feel that it is important to say, "How did you get it?" If you said you used random numbers, that is a piece of information that would not affect my prior. On the other hand, if you say you got this sample by standing on the street corner counting everyone who passed between 12:00 and 1:00, I would say that affects my prior.

Let me summarize. It seems that one can provide a formal justification within the Bayesian framework for randomization by simply observing that the way in which the sample was obtained is information in the same sense that observations of sample members is information and will influence the priors with which one started. There are certain ways of obtaining samples that would result in such priors where you could not possibly draw any sharp conclusions from samples obtained in that way.

In such situations, randomization would lead to sharper conclusions and is in that sense justifiable within the Bayesian framework.

· *Meyer*: When you say, "Depending on the way the sample is drawn, this might influence your prior," are you speaking of a prior on an underlying parameter?

· *Cornfield*: I'm thinking of the specific situation of sampling a finite population and, in principle, one has a prior distribution of the value that one is going to measure on each individual. Once one makes the observation on the individual, that prior is compared to a posterior which is spiked at the value. But, there is an intermediate stage when one considers how the individuals entered the sample. We may have sampled by standing on a street corner and taking the first fellows that went by. I have some knowledge of the way the world works, and the people who walk by this corner at this time tend to be different from other people. My prior has been changed, and it may be changed in such a way that no matter how many such people you took in your sample, you would be unable to reach any sharp conclusions. If that were the case, it is a bad way to do a sample.

· *Mallows*: I am not clear what sort of a prior you are considering because you are specifying a prior for the observation on every possible individual. These have to be dependent in some way, otherwise any observations you make will not affect the distributions on the other individuals at all.

· *Cornfield*: There are various ways of inducing this dependence. One way that I have found useful is to say that each individual has a prior from a given family with one or more unspecified parameters. Suppose the priors were all normal with an unknown mean. We put a prior on the mean and this produces a dependence to the observations. But I certainly couldn't carry that program forward if I had a very biased method of sampling, because then I would have to say the priors on the individuals in the sample have now been changed to posteriors which are different from those outside the sample. There are particular situations in which biased methods of sampling could make so big a change that you would say this is a poor way of getting information.

I don't see any fundamental contradiction between the Bayesian approach and randomization, though this rough idea needs a lot of careful working out. The basic difference is that the frequentist can't get started unless he randomizes because he can't get a sampling distribution. This is a very fundamental thing for him, and in fact I have had statisticians ask how inferences can be drawn from observational surveys, like ones on smoking and health, mortality for smokers and nonsmokers. They want to randomize between these two groups, and they ask how can the statistician regard this as a proper subject for statistical analysis. That seems to be a pathological point of view for a frequentist to take.

· *Mallows*: It seems to me the crucial question in all this is what you think the proper reference set is.

· *Cornfield*: Yes.

· *Mallows*: I think a Bayesian ought to say no.

· *Cornfield*: Well I say yes in that I recognize the concept.

· *Mallows*: Statistical inference is concerned with recognizing certain observations as being one of a population and trying to infer something about the population from this individual. The basic assumption is that this individual represents the population or is randomly drawn from this population.

· *Cornfield*: If I made any single point in my paper, it is that in attempting to apply frequency ideas one flounders on identifying the appropriate reference set. An observation can be identified with many possible reference sets, and the conclusion you draw depends on the reference set that you regard as appropriate. I ended up this paper with a very pointed remark from Keynes written almost 50 years ago in which he makes this his basic criticism of the frequency probability.

· *Mallows*: I didn't think it was a criticism of the frequency approach. It is a basic difficulty in statistics. You have to decide how wide you want your inferences to be. If you want to make all your judgments on the basis of your personal opinions at the time, then you go ahead and do that. If you are willing to state only that you are going to regard this thing as a random sample from this population, then you do something like estimating a parameter.

· *Cornfield*: Let's take the classical case of where a choice of reference sets may affect what conclusion one draws from a set of data, the usual case of sampling from the binomial or from a negative binomial. In one case a number of events is fixed, and in the other case the number of successes is fixed. Now the frequentist may in fact draw different conclusions from a given r and a given n, depending on which reference set he regards appropriate but the Bayesian won't.

· *Mallows*: That is where I have difficulty. You use the word conclusions. Now what does the Bayesian do? He ends up with a posterior distribution for the p. That is his conclusion?

· *Cornfield*: Let us say it is the posterior and anything derivable from the posterior, like the mean of the posterior, or a 95 percent interval.

· *Mallows*: Suppose an action follows, and I decide to act as though my hypothesis were true. Don't you think it is relevant to ask what the frequency characteristics of this whole procedure are?

· *Cornfield*: One would introduce utilities for various actions conditional on various values of p and then take the average value of this utility function averaged over the posterior. Let's behave in such a way as to minimize it, and since the posterior won't depend on the reference set, neither will the average of the utility or of the cost function averaged over the posterior. So the Bayesian's behavior will be influenced by his priors, by his utility functions, by his observations, but not by the reference set that he regards the observation is imbedded in.

· *Mallows*: Certainly if we can formalize our problems in a decision theory way, I don't believe anyone would disagree with the analysis.

· *Lindley*: What do you do this for if not to make decisions?

· *Mallows*: To learn.

· *Lindley*: Why do you want to learn?

· *Mallows*: Are you saying that statistics is decision theory or decision theory is statistics? I disagree with that.

· *Lindley*: I was going to take you up on this remark in your paper. "The statistician's role is that of attorney and not that of judge." He is in the role of judge, very much so, in the sense that somebody has got to be the judge and that judge ought to be jolly well informed on statistics if he is going to do his job properly.

· *Mallows*: He has to be informed. It is his job in a professional capacity to summarize the data in a way in which the information can be understood.

· *Lindley*: If you want to summarize the data, that's all right. Just calculate a posterior distribution. But it is the statistician's job as judge to carry the job on a little further by calculating from the posterior distribution certain things that are relevant in this situation. If, for example, the judge has got to make the decisions, guilty or not guilty, to simplify the situation, then, he is going to have quite a problem passing from his posterior distribution to his decision. The way I see it, it is the statistician's job to help him do this. And what ought to be quoted is the posterior probability that this man is guilty.

· *Mallows*: I am just distinguishing the statistician from the decision maker. It seems to me that there are certain problems in the analysis of data that are distinct from . . . .

· *Lindley*: But I don't believe you can analyze data without reference to the decision that may be made about it. You can do this analysis, but it is, generally speaking, so complicated to express all the facets of the data that one would be deterred from doing that, and if one can possibly relate it to a particular problem, the thing becomes so much easier.

· *Cornfield*: I used to have much stronger views on the dichotomy than I do now. I used to think that there was a clear-cut distinction between inference-based procedures and decision-based procedures. I believe now that the major distinction is that there are some problems in which the alternative actions and courses involved in taking them are so complicated and so beyond the competence and perhaps the ability of the statistician to specify, that he seeks a situation in which he cannot be involved and summarizes his observations in some useful way, ordinarily in a posterior. He makes himself available to a decision maker who is more willing to stick his neck out in these matters. I don't see any real conflict between the man who stops with an inference and the man who goes on to make a decision—it just depends on the circumstances.

If I may say one word in reference to an example I had in my paper—the problem of decision making in clinical trials. There is an ethical problem in clinical trials in the sense that you have a new form of therapy established, and a question is whether it is ethical to do an experiment on human beings. That everybody is uneasy about this is indicated by the fact that nobody calls it an experiment. They always call it a trial. The usual justification for conducting such an experiment is that you don't know which therapy form is better at the beginning. You are not really being unfair to any patient, and that has a certain cogency, until you get your first observation. You now have an observation and one of them appears a little better than the other. As far as the next patient is concerned, the best thing for him is to put him on what appears to be the better therapy. We attempted to formalize this by generalizing a little bit from work that Frank Anscombe and Ted Colton had done on the problem like this in which, roughly speaking, what one tries to do is maximize the number of patients assigned to the superior therapy over the course of a two-stage procedure. Now I've been talking to a number of doctors, all of whom are very negative to this approach, and the general feature of the approach is that as data accumulates you allocate more and more of your patients to what appears to be the superior therapy in accordance with a formula that follows the specification. They all appear negative though none of them gave me any cogent reasons until the other day, one of them did. I think it illustrates the kind of difficulty you get in with a cost formulation. He said, "Well, this might in fact be a reasonable way for a physician to behave as the physician is not only concerned with the next patient, but the next batch of patients, and if you have a criterion that will maximize over the next batch of patients, that's all right." But, he said, "We also have to get the consent of the patient. This is a legal requirement, and it seems like an ethical requirement, and in fact, the legal requirement is that he give *informed* consent. Now informed consent in principle must mean that he knows as much as you do. He knows the results of the trial, and if he does, he has a different cost function or different utility function than you. He is not concerned with the next batch of patients, he is concerned only with himself." So, if you try to follow this through to its logical conclusion, it turns out that the physician has one cost function and the patient has another cost function.

· *Mallows*: You try to get patients who are sufficiently public-spirited that they will take the physician's cost function.

· *Cornfield*: I'm not one such patient. I think there was a little bit to be said along those lines in the sense that if a patient really thinks about it, he is concerned not only with therapy for himself but at least for the members of his immediate family. He has some sort of personal interest in accumulating some knowledge but he is much less interested than others who are involved in the enterprise. The cost formulation, when you try to apply it to such a situation, gets difficult, but not difficult for any reasons you know that are inherent in the Bayesian approach. It gets difficult because life is difficult.

· *Meyer*: Could we return to this issue of randomization? There seem to be two thoughts on this in the field of education. One is that we'd better have random samples because we don't know how to do tests of significance, etc., otherwise. The other view is that it is difficult to obtain random samples in practical school situations, but that we could measure the students before the study on certain variables, say IQ. Then using our knowledge of how IQ is related to the criterion, we might go ahead with an analysis. How might the Bayesian tackle this?

· *Cornfield*: It seems to me that what the Bayesian does is to formalize what good scientific practice is. Theory is no substitute for sound data. If you have data whose soundness is suspect, good scientific practice consists of asking in what ways could we possibly go wrong by using this suspicious set of data, and the formal equivalent of this is considering classes of priors that one might assign in view of the method by which the data is collected. The Bayesian helps because he formalizes this, but he doesn't turn a sow's ear into a silk purse.

One of the health agencies in Washington was concerned with accumulating a lot of experience about long-term effects of using birth control pills. We all know how you design such a study—you would allocate women at random into one group that used the pills and a group that didn't, and you follow them. This doesn't seem like a very practical way of going at it and so the proposal was to follow two groups of women, one of whom had decided to use the pills and the other who had decided not to use the pills. What does one do in such a situation? One tries to think how such women might differ, one tries to get as many measurements as one can think of that might bear on this difference, and the formalization of the whole process is in a sense that you are groping for appropriate prior distributions to assign in view of the way these two groups were formed, but none of these is substitute for a better experiment if you can possibly do it.

· *Meyer*: Are you implying that the better experiment is one that is randomized?

· *Cornfield*: Well, in this situation I would say that if I had a clear-cut choice between these two alternatives, women selecting themselves into these two groups or assignment by random procedure, I would prefer the second.

· *Lindley*: Suppose that we have a group of students and that we are considering two teaching methods. One method of experimentation will be to divide those students into two groups by some random mechanism and to teach one of those groups by one method and the other group of students by the other method. But then, nobody would do that in practice because one would ask if there were any real difference between these students that might affect the situation. If one has a very heterogeneous group of students, some with high intelligence and some with low intelligence, then you would do some sort of matching. You would control the experiment by selecting a pair of bright students, giving one of the bright students one teaching method and the other bright student the other teaching method. In other words, you would block the experiment on this factor. Indeed, I say that a good experiment designed in this situation would block on every factor that you thought was relevant. You are blocking on your prior knowledge, and you are not going to randomize if you have any significant piece of prior knowledge about these students. Then you might randomize on the remaining situation as far as one could.

· *Cornfield*: Why do you say "might"?

· *Lindley*: Well you might because it is just a convenient way of doing it, but I don't see any objection really to sitting down and allocating them without randomization in any way. You might take these students and allocate them on the basis of the initial of their surname. It would not be a random procedure, but it might be all right. I once suggested doing this back at home on an educational experiment of this sort when it was concerned with teaching Welsh. Somebody said to me, "You know, that would be terrible if you did it like that because by far the commonest surname in this particular district is Jones, and all the Jones' are Welsh, and so if you allocated them in this way you would get more Welsh in your first method than you would in the other." So I said to myself, "That is sure right. Now I've got to block on this factor which I hadn't thought about before; but when I've exhausted all these things, then I can just put these students into these classes in any way I like." You can see there is another way round, because if you did randomization and it came up to be one of these funny randomizations, one that put all the males in the first group and all the females into the second, you would say to yourself, "My goodness that's ridiculous, I'll randomize again." The better procedure would have been to take the males and the females and block according to sex and do that experiment. I don't see that there is any need, whether you are a Bayesian or a non-Bayesian, in using a table of random numbers to design an experiment.

· *Cornfield*: I am not sure that I am in agreement with you on this. I don't think it is a Bayesian or non-Bayesian issue. I think it is a question of how confident you are that you understand all the factors involved.

· *Geisser*: That's right. That there aren't biases in the selection of factors that you haven't thought about.

· *Cornfield*: In most of the situations that statisticians are involved in, they are not deeply familiar with the variables involved, and they depend on somebody else to tell them what the variables are, and as just a good piece of scientific practice, it is well to be skeptical of the collaborators. They may not know as much as they seem to. The way to safeguard against this, after you have taken care of everything that can be introduced into the situation, is to randomize.

· *Geisser*: Would you say this plays the same part as a double blind?

· *Cornfield*: Yes, it is the same sort of thing. It is a way of eliminating certain conceivable sources of error that you don't know enough to specify. I don't see that this is an anti-Bayesian way to behave.

· *Geisser*: But the point, of course, is that it eliminates them in a frequentist sense over possible samples that you never get.

· *Cornfield*: No, because I would formalize it Bayesianwise and say that the prior distributions that I have for the individuals in the two groups are essentially the same.

· *Lindley*: But if I had allocated these students in what seemed to me some reasonable way, I would still have the same prior distribution.

· *Cornfield*: You might change your prior in the light of subsequent information, in the light of the knowledge that the Jones' are Welsh. Of course, that can also happen with randomization. You might randomize and get all your Jones' in one group. I suspect you are going to change your priors in the light of future information less often, if you randomize, than otherwise.

· *Hill*: Let me pose a question. Suppose on different occasions you are driving in your car and your wife asks you which is north and which way is south and each time you want to go north but each time you go south. These are very different occasions and you seemed to have missed out on every chance you had. It is going to happen once again, and so you think things over and decide which way you think is north and then you recollect that every time you decided, you were wrong, so you say, I'd better do the opposite. On the other hand, if you try to do the opposite, then the same thing still applies. If you were going to do that, you would still be wrong. Is it a solution to flip a coin? Your experience is that you have been wrong every time. If you flip a coin, the probability is a half that you'll be right or wrong. There are only two choices, north or south. Should you randomize, i.e., flip the coin, or should you decide the same way as you have been doing previously?

To make the problem a little more natural, suppose you had n pairs of twins, and you assigned each member of a twin pair to either a control or a treatment group—nonrandomly. Now suppose you learn that in each of your first n decisions the healthier twin was assigned to the treatment group and you were biasing the experiment in some way that you don't understand very well. On the next pair, should you flip a coin for the assignment to treatment or control, or should you make the decision in the same way you have in the past? Randomization is a very subtle problem for Bayesian and non-Bayesian alike. I tend to agree with Professor Lindley about blocking. You have to take into account all the prior knowledge you have on the things that you think are important and block accordingly. But after you have blocked as much as you can, should you randomize? A pure Bayesian says it does no good—it may not do any harm—but it certainly doesn't do any good as far as the informativeness of the experiment because randomization is irrelevant to the true quantities and so you make the same inference whether you randomize or not, but on the other hand I suggest this other difficulty that I experienced about being wrong n times out of n.

· *Lindley*: I'm not sure it is the same sort of problem. I'm trying to capture the spirit of this paper of De Finetti's—Are there good probability appraisers or not? I might learn from my previous experience of plotting prior distributions. For example, I might put a prior distribution on a binomial parameter and later I learn what the parameter was. I keep going over this operation for a while and I say to myself, "Well, Lindley, old fellow, you've got a bias." It seems that I turn all these small worlds, all these individual binomials, and that I would put them together, and then say that I've learned something about the way I'm working. I've got to jack my probability up and I think I would do that. I would learn that I am a bad probability appraiser and would try to correct it and make myself a good one.

· *Hill*: I think there is a logical dilemma in that. Your argument would perhaps lead to the following. Let's treat these things as an ordinary Bernoulli sequence and you have these n out of n failures. Maybe your posterior probability, that no matter what you are going to do is going to be wrong the next time, is n out of n plus 1. That's what I believe is the kind of argument you are giving. You have a very high probability that whatever you do is going to be wrong, because you do it on your own judgment . . . .

· *Lindley*: I wouldn't have the feeling that something malevolent is working against me.

· *Geisser*: I wonder if one in your situation shouldn't try to find out why he has gone wrong all these n times.

· *Cornfield*: Is there a problem of relevant sets here? You have your past experience and one way you can interpret it is that no matter what you do, you're wrong, and does that statement include randomization as well?

· *Hill*: You would surely calculate the probability to be one half that the next time you were going to be right if you flipped the coin.

· *Cornfield*: I would certainly regard this as a different subset. In fact, you would have the same difficulty if you excluded that and said, "The first six times that I confused north and south was because I used a compass, and the next six times I looked at a map." Do you want to combine these two experiences?

· *Geisser*: I'm not exactly sure, Bruce, what relevance this has to experimental randomization.

· *Hill*: The point that I am trying to make is that there is a lot to be understood about randomization even from a Bayesian point of view, and I would certainly not recommend to educational people and psychologists that they dispense with randomization, apart from the blocking business which we all agree about. I think not only is there this dilemma to be resolved, but there is also the question of group decision making in which different people have different prior opinions. Randomization may have some value from that point of view also.

· *Lindley*: My feeling of group decision making is that there is no real trouble over the priors. If a group of people is going to make a decision, they can start off with different priors, but if they talk enough they resurrect the old data they are using, and I would be very much surprised if they didn't get to very similar priors in the end. But what does bother me is, how are you going to resolve the conflict between the alternatives? If we, as a committee, have to make a decision, and one of us has an entirely different utility function from the others, I don't see how to proceed. It seems to me to be one of the major problems in civilization. The major problem in civilization is how you reconcile completely different utilities when one course of action has got to be taken.

· *Cornfield*: I'm not willing to dismiss this disagreement on priors that easily. If one considers the process by which a scientific consensus is formed on a problem, there are many problems one can look at in science in which equally well informed people, equally aware of the evidence available, come to quite different conclusions. The formalization of the fact that they come to different conclusions is that they had quite different priors. Take the example of smoking and mortality. There are some people who think there is nothing to it. Most people, who are equally familiar with the evidence, think there is something to it, and if you try to investigate the reasons for these differences, the people who don't think there is anything to it have a strong prior that people who decide to smoke are different in some basic genetical constitutional way.

· *Lindley*: They must have some evidence for this. They ought to be able to produce it.

· *Cornfield*: They haven't and this leads me to say they simply have different priors.

· *Geisser*: Fisher produced what he thought was evidence but other people disagreed.

· *Cornfield*: I would agree that the difference in utilities is a major problem in group decision making. I think the difference in priors will often explain a confused and contradictory state of opinions in science for quite a long period of time.

· *Lindley*: Scientists are not Bayesians at the moment. We statisticians have made a tremendous discovery that people ought to change their opinion according to Bayes' theorem. There is quite a bit of empirical evidence to show that people don't do this. They tend to change their odds conservatively as compared with the change calculated by Bayes' theorem.

· *Meyer*: We might get to some of the technical points that were raised on the papers. Could we start with you, Dr. Mallows?

· *Mallows*: I would like to ask about Professor Hill's analysis of the components of variance problem. He claims that the Bayesian analysis is in violent disagreement with all previous frequentist analyses. You have a mean square between which has an expectation, $\sigma^2 + J\sigma_\alpha^2$ and a mean square within which has expectation, σ^2, so the estimate, $\hat{\sigma}_\alpha^2$, is obtained by subtracting MSW from MSB and dividing by J. The peculiar situation arises when MSW is greater than MSB, and the unbiased estimate is negative.

The ratio of mean squares, under the random model, is $1 + J(\sigma_\alpha^2/\sigma^2)$ times an F statistic. The observation is that the ratio of mean squares is considerably smaller than one. I would infer that σ_α^2/σ^2 is small, but this is different from saying σ_α^2 is small. Small relative to what? There is no contradiction in saying σ_α^2 is small and σ^2 is large, but that says nothing about how big σ_α^2 is.

· *Hill*: Are you trying to argue that it is conceivable that the classicalist could come up with a reasonable result? It is a fact that no one did.

· *Mallows*: You have made a large contribution in saying that the way in which σ^2 gets large and σ_α^2/σ^2 gets small is exactly so that you end up by knowing nothing about σ_α^2. In fact it is just flat. But I don't see where the frequentist would have said that σ_α^2 is small. All he would have said is that this ratio is small. That is in agreement with what you say.

· *Hill*: Fisher says that the fiducial probability is nearly one that σ_α^2 is zero in that situation. Those frequentists who have spoken about the problem have concluded that if the model were not rejected, they would infer that σ_α^2 is small.

· *Mallows*: Small relative to what?

· *Hill*: Some of them say it's zero; like 1 in a light-year, just a small number in whatever units were being used. The prior distribution determines the meaning of "small" in any real problem.

· *Lindley*: I'd like to explore with Dr. Mallows why he wants to calculate these curves towards the end of his paper. To put it another way, why he wants to calculate these risk functions. As Cornfield has impressed on us, the inference ought not to depend on the sampling scheme that gives rise to the data, and yet here we have somebody calculating quantities which depend on the sampling scheme. If the sampling scheme changed, he'd get different ones. And so, the first feeling I have is that these things are far outside the Bayesian canon. Why do you feel that they are useful things to look at?

· *Mallows*: Because I am in a situation where I have some unknown parameters and I am trying to get some idea where the values actually lie—in the case for which I have data. Various procedures have been published. Each kind of prior that might be assumed leads to a procedure for saying where these parameters might be. I am interested in comparing the different procedures.

· *Lindley*: But your judgment of these procedures is based on what would happen if you repeated this thing over and over again; when in fact, what one is going to do is to do it once only. Therefore, you have to make a major decision as to what the repetition is, and I just can't see what relevance this has.

· *Mallows*: This comes back to the basic question as to what your reference set is. The Bayesian is willing to say that the only relevant reference set is what the other values are at the time which you might have taken into account, whereas I think the random mechanism that gives rise to the data given the parameter is certainly something that has to be specified before you can get off the ground, so why not use that? It is in some sense a relevant probability mechanism.

· *Lindley*: We both agree that you have to specify the probability of the observations. Where we are disagreeing is the probability of the observation that we didn't get. You won't specify them and I don't.

· *Mallows*: Why worry about the specifications of parameters if they aren't the ones you are going to get?

· *Cornfield*: We know the observations.

· *Geisser*: It does not pertain to the observations you have obtained.

· *Mallows*: What I am doing here is comparing procedures before seeing the data.

· *Lindley*: If you are comparing the procedures in advance, then we are on a different wicket because the Bayesian will not look at the risk function that you are looking at. He would look at the procedures to see whether or not the sampling plan of the scheme being proposed was a good one or not, and he would do a pre-posterior analysis.

· *Mallows*: Why not investigate the effect of different priors?

· *Lindley*: No! He has a fixed prior.

· *Mallows*: I am not going to say this is my prior, that I believe in this prior and nothing can shake me from it.

· *Lindley*: We are all prepared to be shaken from our priors when we go out and collect data.

· *Mallows*: I just want to know how important the different assumptions might be. How they would influence my actions. This is a study of robustness, if you like.

· *Lindley*: The key question is why should you investigate your prior through these risk functions? I do a Box type robustness analysis, work out what the posterior is for the different priors and see. If it had changed terrifically with the prior then I would realize I would have to make some serious decision.

· *Mallows*: You say that a Bayesian estimate is a description of a posterior, so I am studying how that parameter of the posterior varies with choice of prior.

· *Lindley*: But you're seeing how it changes over the different samples. The way I want to do it is to look at it for a fixed sample.

· *Hill*: Let me comment on a point in Professor Lindley's paper. If you look at equation 16, you see that apart from the cost of observations, he is going to be led to include every variable in sight in the prediction. This would be true not only if the costs were literally zero but also if they were sufficiently small. I am not opposed to the introduction of costs, but it doesn't seem that the inferential question here depends on the costs. It should not depend on the costs in this way. It would not be a good idea in general to include every variable in sight even with no costs. You've got n plus 1 points. I don't see how you are led away from fitting an nth degree polynomial to n plus 1 points, except by means of your costs.

· *Lindley*: I agree the problem of fitting a polynomial to data is one that at the moment I can't fit in very conveniently to the Bayesian analysis. I have prior belief in the smoothness of the polynomial. We need to express this idea quantitatively, but I don't know how to do it. We could bring in our prior opinion that some of these regression coefficients are very small.

· *Hill*: If you did that in the way you mention later, isn't it true that if costs were literally zero, you would wind up fitting everything in sight. Unless you said they were literally zero with prior probability one.

· *Mallows*: I have a formulation which is a frequentist one in which what I did was look at the sum of the mean square error of the fitted regression function summed over the data points. You take the difference between the estimated regression function and the true one, square it, and take the expected value of that. I compare different procedures for estimating the regression function on the basis of what the expected value of this thing is. That seems to me to be relevant and it makes me unhappy with the answer that says you ought to put everything in. It's certainly not a Bayesian outlook, is it?

· *Hill*: It is clear that if you were to take this answer of putting everything in, you would be going against the accumulated experience of people who have been fitting things for many years.

· *Lindley*: You must remember that the variance here is assumed known, so this has an effect on the issue. If the variance is unknown, then you wouldn't get a conclusion like this because there would come a point when the loss of degrees of freedom would matter. I mean, I wouldn't fit the polynomial for every point because that would give an estimate of variance which is zero.

· *Hill*: This is one of Jeffreys' main problems in his book *Theory of Probability*, to try and somehow get away from this.*

· *Lindley*: He does this in a way I don't like too much. He puts a probability that makes him reluctant to introduce each parameter in turn. But I am not at all enamored of this idea that we have to order the parameters even with a polynomial—the linear term first, the square term next, etc. Why should it be in that particular order? The point is that in a Bayesian analysis cost-free observations are always worth having.

· *Meyer*: This is related to an issue we talk about in education and psychology, namely the problem of cross validation. We go out and obtain some variables and fit a multiple regression equation. We want that equation to have a good fit in the next sample. Is it possible to include too many variables so that we would actually do worse in the second sample than if we had deleted some of these small ones in the first sample and then used the reduced equation with the second sample?

· *Lindley*: If they are cost free, you should just use them. I don't see how they can do you any harm.

· *Meyer*: So your answer would be "No," that including more variables, even though they were very small, would probably do better for me in the cross validation on the second sample?

· *Mallows*: I disagree.

· *Hill*: I do, too.

· *Cornfield*: So do I.

· *Lindley*: I don't have any strong grounds for my feeling except that my accounts are formulated in such a way that this happens.

· *Hoadley*: In one time series problem that I know of the author used

---

* Jeffreys (1961).

an auto regression model. His predictions were worse than when he did some kind of reasonable fit.

· *Mallows*: Worse in a sort of predicted mean square error sense.

· *Hoadley*: His predictions turned out worse when he was actually able to observe what he was predicting. In other words, overfitting led to poor predictions.

· *Lindley*: Let's suppose that he had taken some data that was generated from a Markoff process of the first order and we don't know this. We do the fitting and bring in every term, say, about to the sixth order. Then I go and compare the results with what actually happened. If indeed it is first order, I would have done better to have used a prediction of the first order in hindsight. But I don't see that invalidates bringing them all in because with the prior information that I had, I didn't know it was the first order.

· *Mallows*: But the situation you are actually in is that when you see the data you are not really sure whether you should have six or fifteen.

· *Lindley*: That's right, that's why I want to bring them all in.

· *Mallows*: Are you always going to lump for the biggest number?

· *Lindley*: I'm going to bring them all in if they are cost free.

· *Mallows*: What do you mean cost free? We just have the data. We can use any prediction form we like.

· *Lindley*: We will use them all, then.

· *Mallows*: But if you do that then your predictions will be worse than if you used a small number.

· *Lindley*: I would guess it would only be worse if the data, in fact, was of a small order.

· *Hoadley*: I think it should be pointed out here that one method that was used for choosing variables was spectral analysis. Spectral analysis suggested certain lags, and using these lags worked better than using all the lags.

· *Lindley*: It's not clear why a Bayesian should use the lower order. He would have high opinions about the use of these particular lags, but it seems to me that even if the dependence on the other lags was terribly tiny, I don't quite see how he loses anything other than the extra computing labor in bringing them in. The gain might be infinitesimal, but if it's epsilon at no cost then you have the epsilon.

· *Cornfield*: Suppose we are interested in a set of parameters σ_1 and σ_2, and we have independent observations—t_1's distribution depends on σ_1, t_2's distribution depends on σ_2, etc., to t_n—and now in some sense we want to estimate this vector. Suppose that the situation is that some of the t's are near zero. The intuitive feeling that a number of us have been expressing is that there must be some formulas that would tell you to estimate the σ's. The question is, are there appropriate formulas? I conjecture, and I conjecture in my paper, that if one assigned a multivariable prior to these things with correlation coefficients which in turn were assigned some very diffuse prior distribution and if one carried that analysis through, that it would in fact tell you to take the t's that are closest to zero and move your estimates of the σ's even closer to zero. And this is only a small extension again of what you said in discussing Stein's paper, the only difference being that you said assign independent priors.

· *Lindley*: In the analysis in my paper, the expectation of those σ's would have to be literally zero before I would not include them.

· *Cornfield*: What kind of a prior was assigned in this case?

· *Lindley*: The analysis is for the uniform independent prior, but Dr. Hill made the point that it would probably persist even if I had the other sort of prior. I think he is right.

· *Cornfield*: Even if they were dependent?

· *Lindley*: I think it will only depend on the mean values of the σ's.

· *Hill*: I think you have to go into this hypothesis type of formulation of Jeffreys'. You have to have in mind a very complex mixture of distributions. Many hypotheses, many prior distributions conditional on the hypotheses, most of them having prior probability epsilon, but then when you get the right kind of data you'll be led in the direction of setting certain σ's zero or nearly zero, and in Lindley's problem, you'll be led away from fitting all the parameters. I think this is quite apart from whether σ^2 is known or unknown.

· *Lindley*: Could we refer to equation (6), which is the analysis for this problem for any data? "H" you remember just describes—it is a symbol that covers the data so it can be any sort of data at this point. There the choice of i depends on the expectation of the σ's given H and, therefore, it doesn't seem to me to matter whether there is a concentration of prior probability on σ equals zero or not. The thing that matters is its mean value, and if its mean value is slightly away from zero and the observation is cost free, then this analysis suggests that you include it, even if the probability of θ being zero given H is .99999. I'm unhappy about this.

· *Geisser*: What you require is the best predictor. You've minimized the squared error. Suppose you had a two-hump distribution with the mean of the posterior distribution in the valley. It would seem rather odd to take that as the predicted value of the observation. That's the mean that minimized the squared error loss but one would feel uncomfortable.

· *Mallows*: Only if one has to play the rules of the game. I would want to say that it is either here or over there.

· *Geisser*: Perhaps predict it in an interval where there is more density.

· *Lindley*: There may be in my formulation of it as a decision problem a fault with it in some way. My formulation here is a point decision.

· *Hill*: But is it true that equation (6) will make you observe everything if all the C_i are zero?

· *Lindley*: I don't know. The point is that it only includes the mean value of σ. And I am sure this is right—there is a paper by Dickey that recently appeared that makes the same point. That is very strongly counter to intuition and it says that the standard errors of these regression parameters just don't matter, and that is surprising by any standard.

· *Meyer*: We have a question for you, Dr. Cornfield. In your paper you talk about sampling to a foregone conclusion, and you deal with this point by using the Jeffreys' type priors where you put a lump of probability at a particular parameter point. When I read Jeffreys I see certain chapters talking about hypotheses where he uses this lump-type prior, and then in other chapters dealing with estimation, he uses a smooth-type distribution. It seems this is an inconsistency.

· *Cornfield*: Well I don't think there is a universal prior that applies in all problems. . . .

· *Meyer*: But suppose in the same problem you are interested in estimation and also in a particular hypothesis.

· *Cornfield*: If you are interested in a hypothesis, then in some sense you are willing to put a lump of probability in at that point. . . .

· *Geisser*: Not necessarily. It might not be a point hypothesis.

· *Cornfield*: Suppose it is. In addition to testing the hypothesis, you want to do estimation. There is no problem. You've specified your prior that leads to a posterior. It is a curious kind of posterior because if you put a lump of prior probability at a point, there is a lot of posterior probability at a point, but then away from that point there is a smooth posterior if you had a smooth prior away from that point. If you want to compute the average of that posterior, you can, and essentially what you do is you get the average of the smooth part of the posterior, and you weight that average by one minus the posterior probability of the hypothesis, then multiply the hypothesis value by the posterior probability of the hypothesis value. When I first read Jeffreys I was bothered by this, too, as it seemed one procedure was used for part of week and another for the balance of the week. But I don't feel it is now.

I even feel the order in which he presents it is right. The general run of problems are, borrowing his sense, estimation problems. You don't single out any special value in the parameter space for special treatment, and so for most problems, it would probably be correct to express your prior point of view by having no lump of probability any place. But there are some problems which Jeffreys calls, hypothesis testing. The nicest example I saw of the situation in which you really want to put a lump of probability at a particular point was written by Professor Lindley in which he was talking about linkage. There is a value that the linkage coefficient has when two genes are from different chromosomes and there is a reasonable probability that this may be the case.

· *Meyer*: Would you comment further on the multiple comparisons problem? A point that has bothered me is that two people with essentially the same data are told to do different things, depending on whether they thought of something in advance of seeing the data. One person must use the wider Scheffé-type interval because he didn't think of doing some comparison ahead of time. This is a switch since the frequentist usually criticizes the Bayesian because of his analysis, depending on what's in his head.

· *Cornfield*: I would agree. There was a period when I was in a sort of multiple comparison phase in my statistical career because I did have this feeling that many data analysts have. If you have a lot of observations and one of them unexpectedly is out from the rest, be cautious. Don't jump to conclusions. The multiple comparison procedure seemed like a very nice way of formalizing this. Many statisticians were attracted by this point of view. It has some terrible consequences as you point out which the more you think about the less you can live with. I am going to specify a class of contrasts, then I will consider a composite statement which includes statements on every one of these contrasts. I am going to count myself wrong if any single statement is wrong, and all I want is the chance of being wrong to be some small number. The result depends on the contrast you put into the composite statement and so two people at different ends of the hall could define the contrast in different ways. For example, use Scheffé's method if you want the set of all linear contrasts defined by the analysis of variance, or Tukey's method if you are interested only in paired differences. Given the same set of data with those two different points of view, one would come out with different conclusions about the difference between μ_1 and μ_2, and I remarked that this seemed to me simply another example of the dependence of frequentist procedures on specification of the relevant sample space. It is a very serious dependence for the analysis of data.

There is nothing that prevents a Bayesian from making a probability statement in the form of an interval, but the formalization of the distrust in outlying results comes about in a much more natural fashion using Bayesian methods. It comes about by specification of the nature of the priors that one has on any individual σ's; and most happily this is a prior with unknown parameters which can be influenced by the actual data before you. If with a set of unknown means, you specified that they had a common normal prior with unknown mean and unknown variance, and then you make some observations, you look at how much these observations differ. It is intuitively very clear that this tells you a lot about the variance of this prior.

· *Geisser*: Jerry, it has been my feeling that the main thing wrong with multiple comparisons was what was essentially wrong with the Neyman–Pearson procedure in that you had to fix α beforehand. The Bayesian can take a joint posterior distribution with these σ's and do with them whatever he pleases, like marginals, functions of them, etc. and make his inference on these. I suppose if you use certain indifference priors you almost come out to the same sort of distributions. The pivotal quantities would probably be just about the same; but in one technique you are forced because of that fixed α to do one thing and in the other technique it is almost like Fisher's least significant difference. . . .

· *Cornfield*: Fixing the α's is a difficulty, Tukey remarks on it; but first of all it is a difficulty common to both univariate and multivariate procedures from a frequentist outlook whereas the necessity of the dependence of the inference and the chosen set of contrasts is unique in the multiparameter case. There have been ways suggested by nonfrequentists, to be sure, out of this dependence on preselection of an α. Allen Birnbaum once had a paper in which he said, essentially, compute confidence limits for different confidence coefficients. . . .*

· *Geisser*: You get a confidence distribution.

· *Cornfield*: Yes. I don't seen any reason, in principle at least, why you couldn't do this in more than one dimension. The frequentist interpretation would be a little unclear, but even if one did that, the nature of the multiparameter distribution that one ended up with would depend on a preselected set of contrasts.

· *Geisser*: Suppose you find the posterior of a number of σ's. What do you do with it as a Bayesian? You might find the marginal distribution of a particular contrast and make an inference from that. Perhaps you are not interested in that to start with, but you are interested in it now

---

* Birnbaum (1961).

because you have seen something. It is still legitimate to do this, but it is illegitimate to do this from the other point of view. However, you could be using the same sorts of distributions, pivotal distributions say, in the normal case.

· *Cornfield*: I agree. Bruce made a remark that is relevant along these lines too. In principle you consider every possible set of observations you might get and what you would do with each possible set of observations. But since you are not called upon to estimate the average value of something—error rates or whatever, over some sample space—you do it only for the observations you happen to have.

· *Meyer*: I have some questions for Professor Lindley now. On page 38, the paragraph where you get the marginal. Consider a vector valued parameter, (σ_1, σ_2) and its bivariate posterior distribution. In Bayes, when point estimating σ_1 should I take the mode of the bivariate posterior or the mode of the marginal of σ_1?

· *Lindley*: One shouldn't take any single statistic unless you've formulated it as a decision problem. You have a decision space which, in this case, is one dimensional and a parameter space which is two dimensional. The loss function may be just $(d-\sigma_1)^2$, in which case I would take the mean of the distribution of σ_1. With some other loss function I might take the mode, but I don't think any single statistic ought to be used. I think this is something we have inherited from the classical approach. What I would like to do in this case is to give the whole of that marginal distribution of σ_1. It might be convenient to describe it by its mode and its second derivative.

· *Meyer*: Another question, Professor Lindley. In the decision theoretic framework, I've always thought of the Bayes recipe as the one with the slack and the minimax recipe as the well-spelled-out one. Could you comment?

· *Lindley*: The general procedure of minimax is clearly nonsense. There are many examples in the literature where the minimax estimate is absurd. There isn't a single example in the literature of a Bayes estimate that is absurd.

· *Mallows*: There is this one by Tiao and Tan*—estimation of a variance component.

· *Meyer*: On page 46, you say, "Where y is the true value." The question is: In what sense is the term, "y is the true value" used in view of the previous statement above that everything to a Bayesian is a random variable?

---

* Tiao and Tan (1965).

· *Lindley*: In the sense that I will predict the one value and then at some later stage, a value will be generated by nature, if you like. It will be observed later on, that is the true value.

· *Meyer*: This refers to page 42. The comment is, I do seem to recall from Lindley's own book (1965) the Bayesian version of the chi-square goodness-of-fit test. Why is Lindley ignoring his own ideas here?

· *Lindley*: Touché. The approach in my book is as follows. I take the data and I group it into a finite number of groups and then the relevant sampling distribution generating the likelihood function is the multinomial, so what I've done there is to turn any likelihood by the divisive grouping into the multinomial likelihood. Now the multinomial likelihood for k classes depends on $(k-1)$ parameters. In other words, the parameter space is of finite dimension, a subset of Euclidian space of a finite number of dimensions. I can put a prior distribution on that space because there are a finite number of parameters. I can talk about any distribution as being a point in this space, and I can put a prior distribution over all the space. But I am only able to do this by grouping the observations. If I take the goodness-of-fit problem without this grouping, then the class of distributions is so wide that it can't be described in finite dimensional space, and I can't describe a convenient prior distribution. For example, if you've got some continuous observations, I have strong prior opinions that the density function is really nice and smooth. I can't express that sort of idea just because my mathematics isn't good enough. That's why I don't think what I did in my book is the answer because it is an approximation due to the grouping.

· *Meyer*: We have a question for Professor Hill. There are many alternatives to the usual model of which your model which leads to negative covariance is one example. As sum of squares within becomes large, posterior belief in the usual model decreases, but should belief necessarily increase in just this one alternative? Shouldn't we just distrust the usual model without necessarily picking another particular model? If so, how does the Bayesian approach add anything to classical analysis which says entertain doubt about the usual model if a negative estimate of σ_α^2 occurs?

· *Hill*: My attitude is that you select alternatives according to your judgment which depends on the particular problem at hand. I think it is much the same as the example I mentioned earlier about Jones being drunk. I've got this quality control thing going on and if it gets out of whack, I start thinking about various hypotheses under which this might have happened. I could have thought about them beforehand but if I didn't, so what? I'll still think about it if the data call for it, and I have to introduce them according to my judgment that there can't possibly be a uniformly best sequence of alternatives to consider for all problems. For one problem, some alternative hypothesis will immediately come to mind. I'll start looking at its posterior probability. For another problem a different hypothesis will come to mind. I certainly don't want to just reject the usual model. I'll never do that. I'll only decide that there is some other one that I favor more given the data.

· *Geisser*: Wouldn't you "entertain doubt"?

· *Hill*: No, I'm sure it's wrong. I'm sure all models are wrong. But I am still going to use the one I like best, and I hope never to find a true one, but until I can think of a better one, I am going to continue to use the one I've got. I don't believe, for example, in this Newtonian question. I don't believe Newtonian mechanics can possibly be right and I don't believe relativity can possibly be right. I would have used Newtonian mechanics in my calculations until somebody pointed out to me that given the data that we've got, the other is a great deal more probable. I'll continue to revise my views according to the data that comes in. I'll never hope to get to any true distribution or any true hypothesis.

· *Lindley*: I must say I feel a little bit worried about this. If I had to make a decision, I suppose I would do what Professor Hill suggests. But something like Kempthorne's significance test, I must say, worries me and makes me feel at very least that it is worth hunting for another model. But I am not sure it doesn't go even deeper than that. Suppose I had to make a decision. Suppose I had to align that telescope on Mars before Einstein came along. According to what you said, the best thing is Newtonian mechanics. I would work out the position and I would know very well it was wrong, and it wouldn't be any good pointing the telescope. It just wouldn't see it. But I don't know where to point the telescope. I know very well I won't get it right.

· *Geisser*: You would know where not to point it.

· *Lindley*: That's right, but you know there is something wrong with the decision process. Is it significant in an important way or a trivial way? If somebody gives me some data and points out the proportion of 1's in the first half of that data is significantly greater than the proportion of 1's in the second half, I say that's just chance. Is Kempthorne's chi-squared significant enough in an interesting way?

· *Hill*: If you could say what you mean by "doesn't fit" we'd have the answer. The very meaning of probability is—these observations were possible. We are talking about discrete data and positive probabilities. There can't be any meaning to the statement, "It does fit or it doesn't fit."

· *Lindley*: You can work out in the Newtonian system the posterior probability that Mars is in a certain position, and it never is.

· *Hill*: You didn't expect to get it right, did you?

· *Lindley*: I didn't expect to get it right, but I didn't expect to consistently get it wrong. This is what will happen.

· *Geisser*: Beyond any reasonable error of measurement.

· *Hill*: This gets circular when we start saying what is a reasonable error. You are going right back into the frequency dilemma. How probable is it that your estimate differs from the true quantity by more than epsilon? Let's use that to define, to say that a frequency probability is meaningful, and we go around in circles.

· *Mallows*: I have the feeling that this is the kind of problem where this answer is a meaningful one, but it doesn't fit into a Bayesian model.

· *Hill*: It suggests you should hunt for other hypotheses which have higher posterior probabilities. If you're smart, you will find one, but I don't see what advantage it is to say, "Now I know this isn't a true model!"

I was curious about this because if you use these diffuse priors and the kind of significance test that you and Box and Tiao (1967) recommended (i.e., you look at a region of high posterior probability, and if the hypothesized value isn't in that region of largest density then you reject the null hypothesis), you will sooner or later reject it when it's true if you take enough data, as Cornfield points out. I really don't see how anyone called a Bayesian can recommend such a test of hypothesis without an alternative.

· *Lindley*: That's what I'm saying. The Bayesian framework seems to have this deficiency that it can't do it, but it ought to be able to do it. The mere fact that I cannot think of an alternative doesn't prevent me from feeling there is an alternative there to be looked for.

· *Cornfield*: It seems to me you are trying to solve a non-mathematical problem by use of mathematical procedures. Bayes' theorem is a mathematical procedure, given a hypothesis base for deciding which point the observations favor. Science is a more difficult and more complicated thing than can be circumscribed by a particular mathematical formulation. It is a problem, but I don't think it is a Bayesian problem.

· *Geisser*: You mean more than science though, you mean just the gaining of knowledge.

· *Mallows*: No, this particular branch of science where you are trying to learn from data. This is a very small part. You are trying to learn from numerical data of a certain kind.

· *Cornfield*: It seems to me that Bruce's position as I understand it is a perfectly reasonable one; one that any good scientist can live with. We have a model and we have some way of looking at the model in the light of data. It is an improbable model, and suggests to us that we are going to have to hunt around for another one. I'm not worried that Bayesian methods aren't going to tell me how to do that.

REFERENCES

Ando, A. and Kaufman, G. M. (1965).
Bayesian analysis of the independent multinormal process—neither mean nor precision known. *Journal of the American Statistical Association*, **60**, 347–58.

Anscombe, F. J. (1953).
Discussion to D. V. Lindley, Statistical inference. *Journal of the Royal Statistical Society*, Series B, **15**, 30–76.

Anscombe, F. J. (1954).
Fixed sample size analysis of sequential observations. *Biometrics*, **10**, 89–100.

Anscombe, F. J. (1963a).
Sequential medical trials. *Journal of the American Statistical Association*, **58**, 365–83.

Anscombe, F. J. (1963b).
Tests of goodness of fit. *Journal of the Royal Statistical Society*, Series B, **25**, 81–94.

Aoki, M. (1967).
Optimization of Stochastic Systems. New York: Academic Press, Inc.

Armitage, P. (1967).
Some developments in the theory and practice of sequential medical trials. *Proceedings Fifth Berkeley Symposium on Mathematical Statistics and Probability*, Berkeley and Los Angeles, Vol. 4, 791–804.

Atkins, H. (1966).
Conduct of a controlled clinical trial. *British Medical Journal*, **2**, 377–79.

Bartlett, M. S. (1965).
R. A. Fisher and the last fifty years of statistical methodology. *Journal of the American Statistical Association*, **60**, 395–409.

Beale, E. M. L., Kendall, M. G. and Mann, D. W. (1967).
The discarding of variables in multivariate analysis. *Biometrika*, **54**, 357–66.

BIRNBAUM, A. (1961).
Confidence curves: an omnibus technique for estimation and testing statistical hypotheses. *Journal of the American Statistical Association*, **56**, 246–49.

BOX, G. E. P. and TIAO, G. C. (1967).
Bayesian Estimation of Means for the Random Effect Model. Technical Report No. 117, Department of Statistics, University of Wisconsin, Madison.

COLTON, T. (1963).
A model for selecting one of two medical treatments. *Journal of the American Statistical Association*, **58**, 388–400.

CORNFIELD, J. (1966).
A Bayesian test of some classical hypotheses—with applications to sequential clinical trials. *Journal of the American Statistical Association*, **61**, 577 – 94.

COX, D. R. (1958).
Some problems connected with statistical inference. *Annals of Mathematical Statistics*, **29**, 357–72.

DEMPSTER, A. P. (1963).
On a paradox concerning inference about a covariance matrix. *Annals of Mathematical Statistics*, **34**, 1414–18.

DE FINETTI, B. (1937).
La prévision: ses lois logiques, ses sources subjectives. *Annales de l'Institute Henri Poincaré*, **7**, 1–68. (English translation in KYBURG, H. E. and SMOKLER, H. E. [1964]. *Studies in Subjective Probability.* New York: John Wiley & Sons, Inc., 93–158.)

DUNNETT, C. W. (1955).
A multiple comparison procedure for comparing several treatments with a control. *Journal of the American Statistical Association*, **50**, 1096–1121.

EDWARDS, W., LINDMAN, H. and SAVAGE, L. J. (1963).
Bayesian statistical inference for psychological research. *Psychological Review*, **70**, 193–242.

FISHER, R. A. (1936).
The use of multiple measurments in taxonomic problems. *Annals of Eugenics*, **7**, 179–88.

FISHER, R. A. (1956).
Statistical Methods and Scientific Inference. London: Oliver and Boyd.

GARDNER, M. (1961).
The 2nd Scientific American Book of Mathematical Puzzles and Diversions. New York: Simon and Schuster.

GARSIDE, M. J. (1965).
The best sub-set in multiple regression analysis. *Applied Statistics*, **14**, 196–200.

Geisser, S. (1964).
Posterior odds for multivariate normal classifications. *Journal of the Royal Statistical Society*, Series B, **26**, 69–76.

Geisser, S. (1966).
Predictive discrimination. *Multivariate Analysis, Proceedings of the International Symposium*. New York: Academic Press, Inc., 149–63.

Geisser, S. (1967).
Estimation associated with linear discriminants. *Annals of Mathematical Statistics*, **38**, 807–17.

Gorman, J. W. and Toman, R. J. (1966).
Selection of variables for fitting equations to data. *Technometrics*, **8**, 27–52.

Grundy, P. M., Healy, M. J. R. and Rees, D. H. (1956).
Economic choice of the amount of experimentation. *Journal of the Royal Statistical Society*, Series B, **18**, 22-55.

Guttman, I. (1967).
The use of the concept of a future observation in goodness-of-fit problems. *Journal of the Royal Statistical Society*, Series B, **29**, 83–100.

Hacking, I. (1965).
Logic of Statistical Inference. Cambridge: Cambridge University Press.

Halperin, M., Greenhouse, S. W., Cornfield, J. and Zalokar, J. (1955).
Tables of percentage points for the studentized maximum absolute deviate in normal samples. *Journal of the American Statistical Association*, **50**, 185–95.

Hill, B. M. (1963).
The three-parameter log-normal distribution and Bayesian analysis of a point-source epidemic. *Journal of the American Statistical Association*, **58**, 72–84.

Hill, B. M. (1965).
Inference about variance components in the one-way model. *Journal of the American Statistical Association*, **60**, 806–825.

Hill, B. M. (1967).
Correlated errors in the random model. *Journal of the American Statistical Association*, **62**, 1387–1400.

Hill, B. M. (1968)
Posterior distribution of percentiles: Bayes' theorem for sampling from a population. *Journal of the American Statistical Association*, **63**, 677–691.

Hill, B. M. (1969).
Foundations for the theory of least squares. *Journal of the Royal Statistical Society*, Series B, **31**, 89–97.

Hills, M. (1966).
Allocation rules and their error rates. *Journal of the Royal Statistical Society*, Series B, **28**, 1–31.

Jacobs, O. L. R. (1967).
Introduction to Dynamic Programming. London: Chapman and Hall.

Jeffreys, H. (1961).
Theory of Probability (3rd ed.). Oxford: The Clarendon Press.

John, S. (1961).
Errors in discrimination. *Annals of Mathematical Statistics*, **32**, 1125–44.

Kempthorne, O. (1966).
Multivariate responses in comparative experiments. In *Multivariate Analysis, Proceedings of the International Symposium*. New York: Academic Press, Inc.

Kerridge, D. E. (1963).
Bounds for the frequency of misleading Bayes inferences. *Annals of Mathematical Statistics*, **35**, 1109–10.

Keynes, J. M. (1921).
A Treatise on Probability, London: Macmillan, ch. VIII.

Lindley, D. V. (1961).
The use of prior probability distributions in statistical inference and decision. *Proceedings, Fourth Berkeley Symposium on Mathematical Statistics and Probability*, **1**, 453–68.

Lindley, D. V. (1962).
Discussion to C. M. Stein, Confidence sets for the mean of a multivariate normal distribution. *Journal of the Royal Statistical Society*, Series B, **24**, 285–87.

Lindley, D. V. (1965).
Introduction to Probability and Statistics. Part 2: Inference. Cambridge: Cambridge University Press.

Lindley, D. V. (1968).
The choice of variables in multiple regression. *Journal of the Royal Statistical Society*, Series B, **30**, 31–53.

Mallows, C. L. (1968).
Choosing a subset regression. (To appear.)

Mosteller, F. and Wallace, D. L. (1963).
Inference in an authorship problem. *Journal of the American Statistical Association*, **58**, 275–309.

Mosteller, F. and Wallace, D. L. (1964).
Inference and Disputed Authorship: The Federalist. Reading, Mass.: Addison-Wesley.

Newton, R. G. and Spurrell, D. J. (1967a).
A development of multiple regression for the analysis of routine data. *Applied Statistics*, **16**, 51–64.

NEWTON, R. G. and SPURRELL, D. J. (1967b).
Examples of the use of elements for clarifying regression analyses. *Applied Statistics*, **16**, 165–72.

OKAMOTO, M. (1963).
An asymptotic expansion for the distribution of the discriminant function. *Annals of Mathematical Statistics*, **34,** 1286–1301.

PRATT, J. W., RAIFFA, H. and SCHLAIFER, R. (1964).
The foundations of decision under uncertainty: an elementary exposition. *Journal of the American Statistical Association*, **59**, 353–75.

RAIFFA, H. and SCHLAIFER, R. (1961).
Applied Statistical Decision Theory. Boston: Harvard Graduate School of Business Administration.

RAMSEY, F. R. (1926).
Truth and probability. Reprinted in *Studies in Subjective Probability*, ed. H. E. Kyburg, Jr., and H. E. Smokler (1964). New York, John Wiley & Sons, Inc.

ROBBINS, H. (1952).
Some aspects of the sequential design of experiments. *Bulletin of the American Mathematical Society*, **58**, 527–35.

ROBERTS, H. V. (1967).
Informative stopping rules and inferences about population size. *Journal of the American Statistical Association*, **62**, 763–75.

SAVAGE, L. J. (1954).
The Foundation of Statistics. New York: John Wiley & Sons, Inc.

SAVAGE, L. J. (1954).
The foundations of statistics reconsidered. Reprinted in *Studies in Subjective Probability*, ed. H. E. Kyburg, Jr. and H. E. Smokler (1964). New York: John Wiley & Sons, Inc.

SCHEFFÉ, H. (1953).
A method for judging all contrasts in the analysis of variance. *Biometrika*, **40**, 87–104.

STEIN, C. M. (1959).
An example of wide discrepancy between fiducial and confidence intervals. *Annals of Mathematical Statistics*, **30**, 877–80.

STEIN, C. M. (1962).
Confidence sets for the mean of a multivariate normal distribution. *Journal of the Royal Statistical Society*, Series B, **24**, 265–96.

STONE, M. (1963).
Robustness of non-ideal decision procedures. *Journal of the American Statistical Association*, **58**, 480–86.

TIAO, G. C. and TAN, W. Y. (1965).
Bayesian analysis of random-effect models in the analysis of variance; I: Posterior distribution of variance components. *Biometrika*, **52**, 37–53.

TUKEY, J. W. (1951)
Quick and dirty methods in statistics. II. Simple analysis for standard designs. *Proceedings Fifth Annual Convention, American Society for Quality Control*, 189–97.

TUKEY, J. W. (1962).
The future of data analysis. *Annals of Mathematical Statistics*, **33**, 1–67.

INDEX

adaptive process, 22
admissability, 39
Analysis of variance, 29, 99
Ando, 52
Anscombe, 14, 18, 22, 42, 105
Aoki, 49
apparent error, 62
Armitage, 19
Aspin, 86
Atkins, 2
auto-regression, 116

Bartlett, 79
Bayes' theorem, 10, 11, 13, 38
Beale, 55
Behrens-Fisher problem, 86
beta distribution, 74
binomial sampling, 103
Birnbaum, 120
bivariate posterior distribution, 121
blocking, 107, 109
bounded prior, 20
Box, 27

choosing between hypotheses, 15
classification loss function in, 63
classification rule, 61
clinical trials, 15, 105, 125
coherent or consistent belief, 11, 43
Colton, 23, 105
component of variance, 27, 112
composite proposition, 9, 10

conditional prior, 21
confidence distribution, 120
confidence interval (limits), 25, 86, 87
contrasts, 25, 26
Cornfield, 15, 22
correlated means, 99
cost, 53-54
    minimization of, 23
cost-free observations, 115, 116
Cox, 6, 15, 16
Cp-plots, 54, 92
critical value, 17, 24
cross-validation, 115

decision-based procedures, 105
decision rule, 3, 15
decision theory, 93, 104
DeFinetti, 12, 37, 43, 79, 90
degree of belief, 11
degrees of support, 80
Dempster, 80, 81
Dickey, 118
diffuse prior:
    for covariance matrices, 27
    for variances, 27
    in multivariate normal, 81
discriminant, 59, 61, 68
discriminatory power, 58, 60
distribution-free statistic, 83
Dunnett, 26

empirical error of misclassification, 62
estimation, 118
exchangeable sequences, 43
experimental design, 40

Federalist papers, 18, 71, 73, 93
    discriminant study of, 77
Feiller, 87
fiducial inference, 89
fiducial interval, 86
finite population
    sampling from, 101-2
Fisher, 31, 32, 57, 85, 86, 87, 89
fitting a polynomial, 114, 115
frequentist viewpoint, 2, 3, 6

Gardner, 12
Garside, 55
Geisser, 58, 65, 67, 68, 69
goodness of fit, 35, 42, 74, 91, 94, 95, 96, 97, 122
Gorman, 54

INDEX

Greenhouse, 22
group decision making, 111
Grundy, 40
Guttman

Hacking, 80
Halperin, 22, 26
Healy, 40
Hill, 30, 33, 34, 35, 91, 99
Hills, 58, 63, 67
hypotheses:
    null, 96, 92
    point, 118
    test of, 3, 33, 86, 119, 101
        Bayesian approach, 34
        error rate in, 3

improper prior, 32, 98
incoherent assignment of probability, 12
index errors (in classification), 61, 66
    probability limits on, 64
indifference curves, 16
inference-based procedures, 105
insufficient reason, 79
inverse binomial sampling, 14, 103
irrelevance principle, 80
iterated logarithm, law of, 19

Jacobs, 22
Jeffreys, 34, 37, 73, 90, 96, 98, 115, 118
John, 58
Johnson, 79

Kaufman, 52
Kempthorne, 35
Kendall, 55
Kerridge, 20
Keynes, 28, 103

least significant difference, 120
least squares regression coefficient, 73
likelihood function, 13-16, 35, 73, 83, 89
likelihood principle, 15, 18-20
likelihood ratio test, 35, 36, 78
Lindley, 16, 27, 44, 49, 50, 119, 122
linear discriminant, 57, 66
linear regression, 45, 81
    expected loss in, 46, 53
    quadratic loss in, 46
linkage coefficient, 119
log-normal model, 35
log odds, 77-78

long-run, 5
long-run frequency of errors, 4, 8, 15, 16, 60
loss function, 39, 40, 41, 48
lump-type prior, 118

Mallows, 54, 81, 83, 92
Mann, 55
maximum likelihood estimation, 85, 38, 50
minimax, 121
mis-classification (error)
    confidence limits on, 62
    potential, 70
    predictive error of, 68, 69
    probability of, 60
    unconditional true, 63
model building, 76, 77
Mosteller, 18, 71, 73, 74, 75, 76, 77, 93
multinomial, 122
multiple comparisons, 25, 26, 27, 119, 120
multiple regression, 91, 92
    choosing coefficients in, 81
multistage procedure, 23
multivariate normal distribution, 80
mutually exclusive propositions, 9

negatively correlated residuals, 30, 33
Newton, 54
Neyman-Pearson, 31, 32
non-parametric methods, 42, 91
normal prior, 19, 26
nuisance parameters, 86

Okamato, 67

Pearson, 93
permutability postulate, 80
plotting of residuals, 72, 73
point estimates, 38
Poisson distribution, 74, 76
Pratt, 90
prediction problem, 45, 48
predictive densities of observations, 64, 65
pre-posterior analysis, 113
probability, 9
    conditional, 9-11
    formal properties, 9, 12
    posterior, 11, 13, 38
    prior, 11, 13, 18, 38, 39
proper prior, 98

Raiffa, 40, 90
Ramsey, 11, 90

random experiment, 52
randomization, 101, 106, 107, 108, 109, 110
random model, 29, 33
random sample, 101
reduction in sum of squares in
    multiple regression, 53
Rees, 40
reference set, 103, 104, 110, 113
regression effect, 75
regression, multiple, 91, 92
    standard errors in, 47
    dispersion of estimates in, 47
    choosing coefficients in, 81
regression problems
    prior knowledge in, 55
rejection region, 16
Robbins, 19
Roberts, 15
robust Bayesianism, 83, 93, 114

sample size, 4, 40, 88
sampling to a foregone conclusion, 20, 21, 118
Savage, 12, 16, 34, 37, 79, 87, 90, 91
Scheffé, 26
Scheffés' method, 119
Schlaifer, 40, 90
selection effect, 72, 73, 75
sequential path, 2, 87
sequential testing, 88
sequential t-test, 88
sequential trials, 22
significance level, 4, 6, 24, 87
significance tests, 35, 39, 42, 97
spurrell, 54
Stein, 55, 80, 99, 100, 117
Stone, 81
stopping rule, 14-16, 19-21
student, 26
student's problem
    Bayesian solution, 26
sufficiency, 39, 80
summarization of evidence, 79

Tan, 121
Tiao, 27, 121, 124
Toman, 54
translation invariance, 80
Tukey, 26, 48, 120
Tukey's method, 119
two-armed bandit problem, 22
two-stage sampling, 4-5, 23, 88
Type I and II errors, 88, 16, 17, 3-7
    linear compound of, 16, 17

uniform beta distribution, 75, 76
union, 9, 10
unique sample, 79
utilities, 40, 41, 104

vague prior belied, 22, 30, 80
variance component, 121
  Bayesian inference about, 31
  frequentiest interpretation of, 32
  negative estimate of, 30, 32, 89, 112, 122

Wald, 39
Wallace, 18, 71, 73, 74, 75, 76, 77
weight of evidence, 6, 7
weighted mean squares, 54
Welch, 86

THE BOOK MANUFACTURE

BAYESIAN STATISTICS composition was by Arrowsmith Ltd. Offset printing and binding was by Kingsport Press, Inc. The paper is Perkins and Squier Company's Glatfelter Old Forge. Internal and cover design by John Goetz. The type in this book is Modern.